GROUNDS OF APPEAL

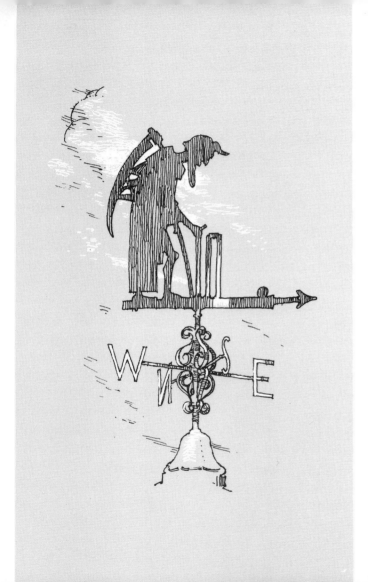

GROUNDS

OF APPEAL

*The Homes of
First-Class Cricket*

*Written and Illustrated by
Aylwin Sampson*

Foreword by
H.R.H. THE DUKE OF EDINBURGH K.G., K.T.

ROBERT HALE   LONDON

ISBN 0 7091 9140 5

Robert Hale Limited
Clerkenwell House
Clerkenwell Green
London EC1R 0HT

Photoset, printed and bound
in Great Britain by
REDWOOD BURN LIMITED
Trowbridge & Esher

This book is dedicated to the memory of
K. A. S. (1903–1979)
who gave me my love of cricket
first at the Angel Ground, Tonbridge,
that nursery of Woolley and Freeman,
sharing with me many days thereafter
at other grounds in Kent

Foreword by

His Royal Highness The Prince Philip,
Duke of Edinburgh, KG, KT

BUCKINGHAM PALACE.

One of the reasons that make it so difficult to explain cricket to foreigners is that they start by assuming that it is just another game. Of course it is a game, but actually playing cricket is only a small fraction of what might be described as greater cricket.

This book illustrates the point very well. It has nothing to do with the game but everything to do with cricket. As a player or a spectator I can remember grounds and pavilions and the whole atmosphere they give to a match long after the scores and even the players have faded from the memory.

I am sure that the mass of information collected in this book will give a great deal of pleasure to all greater cricket fans.

Philip

I doubt if there be any scene in the world more animating or delightful than a cricket-match

Mary Russell Mitford *Our Village* 1832 [the year Thomas Lord died]

Contents

Illustrations

Preface and Acknowledgements

THOUSANDS of people of all ages spend many days each season at cricket grounds. To know something of the past that has given pavilion, stands, trees and indeed the whole backcloth so rich an atmosphere is doubly to enjoy the game.

This then is the aim of this book: to show that great matches, great players leave their mark and give added significance to the places for all who go 'to the cricket'.

Since this book was prepared after the 1979 season, inevitably changes have taken place at many grounds: Trent Bridge has its new Press box, the Oval has renamed its East Terrace the Peter May Enclosure and has a new library, Chesterfield seems certain to lose its County cricket, Scarborough its Fenner Trophy competition.

In attempting to express thanks for help and interest, I am aware of the special mention that can imply indifference elsewhere. However I must take that risk when, after recording the ready response of all Secretaries of the County and University clubs, I thank in particular those of Derbyshire, Essex, Glamorgan, Gloucestershire, Kent, Lancashire, Leicestershire, Northamptonshire, Nottinghamshire, Somerset, Surrey, Sussex, Worcestershire, Oxford and Cambridge. Secretaries, honorary librarians, historians and groundsmen everywhere have freely given me their time, and gone out of their way to show me their grounds and talk of their history.

Past players, writers and commentators have demonstrated that generosity cricket seems to engender and again at the risk of being thought invidious, I would thank especially L. E. G. Ames Esqre CBE, M. C. Cowdrey Esqre CBE, Sir Len Hutton and T. W. Graveney Esqre OBE.

I am also very appreciative of the honour that H.R.H. the Duke of Edinburgh has given to this book by contributing the Foreword.

A.A.S

Introduction

IT IS in cricket above all games that the setting has so much to offer. Through innumerable hours countless people, players, officials, administrators, and spectators, have made the cricket ground their home. By its very nature the time-span of a match permits awareness, a savouring, of the scene. There is opportunity to absorb the character, the atmosphere; memories of past occasions enrich the enjoyment of the present; changes in the game are reflected in its environment; and yet there is a continuity that gives the most humble match a family likeness to the greatest of Tests.

No two grounds are alike: one may be in its county town, another in an industrial city; at the seaside, or under the shadow of a great cathedral; amidst the trees of a park, or surrounded by the spires of some school or college.

Their owners are equally varied. The County Cricket Club, the university authority, a commercial firm, the local council, the Services, a club, even a private trust may be the landlord.

Each ground's history too is different, with some enjoying many decades of total commitment to the game, and others showing evidence of a multitude of uses; many have seen their fortunes subside, to be restored by great team, gifted player or benefactor whose love of the game has been shown in practical ways; others have never wanted.

There is interest, indeed magic, in the names. Even to

those who may never go there, the radio commentary makes "the Kirkstall Lane end" or "Grace Road", "St Lawrence ground" or "the Saffrons" music in the ears of every cricketer.

Maybe we shall never know what the first cricket grounds were, but it is fair to assume that the village green, the local common and the country park have each contributed something to that character which the eighteenth century saw.

Indeed it is through the popularity of landscape painting that our conception of the ideal cricket match owes its genesis.

Admittedly the earlier the picture the less recognizable it is as a cricket field, yet the very emphasis on the open space, however uneven, marks it off from the conventional composition of tree and hedgerow. Spectators are artistically grouped or face the viewer unmindful of the position of the wickets; sometimes liberties with perspective give the players hardly room apparently to swing a bat.

In a view of a match of 1760 at Kenfield Hall, Petham, near Canterbury there seems to be an elementary enclosure, more like a racecourse paddock. The pitch is off-centre; an umpire with his customary bat to lean on is perilously positioned near first slip, though perhaps the presence of two horsemen at third man giving salutation to an old retainer has helped his confidence.

Refreshment tent, a gazebo offering excellent comfort and a large banner bearing a genial "Welcome" have a certain familiarity today. Flags and bunting provide a festive touch that has been perpetuated down the years.

Take as another example, the 1837 engraving of the Grand Jubilee Match at Lord's, where a flag proclaims, not the identity of the teams, but the lessee of the ground, J. H. Dark. Here a pavilion has appeared, yet once again it bears little relation to the pitch. The somewhat meagre crowd have to make do with benches without backs, while once more a horserider seems to invade the field. It is interesting to note the presence of a carriage, subsequently to be so prominent a feature at some Lord's matches, though here the idea of using it as a viewing stand does not seem to have been adopted.

Of the chief figures in these early pictures, their immobility and apparent lack of energetic involvement, the mixture of dress as well as unfamiliar field placing,

---

Although Kent's last County match on the Vine at Sevenoaks was against Sussex in 1829 this ground deserves a place in any account of the development of cricket. For not only is it arguably the oldest ground still in regular use, but it is also associated with the introduction of scoreboards and, more important, the third stump. It was in the match between All England and Hampshire here in 1777 that the new wickets were used to prevent the denial to the bowler of a batsman's dismissal when the ball passed between just two stumps without dislodging the bail.

must appear strange to eyes accustomed to immaculate flannels. Today's players have had their white relieved only by narrow bands on sweater or distinctive colour of cap. Maybe that is the proportion best suited to the background of green, and any alteration will bring visual disaster.

Certainly what the players deny themselves, the ground may profit by; for, like the nautical scene, cricket thrives on that combination of crisp, sparkling white and fresh bright colour in the right proportion. That is why the presence of tents and flags is so import-ant. They have happily performed service as necessary shelter, festive features and identifiers of allegiances. The club colours or county emblem billowing above its pavilion gives the match a significance; to see the echo on each player doubles the assurance.

Thus have the counties marked their emergence. The closing decade of the nineteenth century saw the pattern of the first-class sides established, and it is interesting to note how their contiguity has continued as later counties were admitted. Only Glamorgan stands outside this tight-knit arrangement that ensures that every county shall have its local 'derby'.

The Universities also, strangely, find themselves iso-lated, but there is surely more affinity with the other component of the pattern, namely the country-house ground. The hey-day of that kind of cricket was in Edwardian years, when the great nomadic clubs like I Zingari or Free Foresters would give the game a charac-ter which many a county ground tried to emulate. Striped blazers, strawberries and cream were soon to be found elsewhere, and indeed the blending of the two kinds of ground became more evident as County Cham-pionship matches were played on them.

Today, then, the mixture is rich and varied: there is the county ground, usually but not invariably owned by the county club; then those used for 'weeks' or indi-vidual matches in the county but owned by others. Some counties have made it their policy to play at home in as many different grounds as are suitable, while others have decided, or been forced, to concentrate on one.

This variety of grounds was paralleled by that of sides, not only in personalities but also in status. Some-times the amateurs predominated, other times the pro-fessionals. And in some cases the grounds reflect this. At Hove, for example, you can still see the building for the professional players, at Oxford their meals were taken separately. Indeed in the early years lunch was not pro-

It is at such grounds as the Oval that the atmosphere of Test Match and County Championship dramas can be enjoyed to the full. That the pitch is not on a central axis to the field, and indeed that the term 'oval' does not in fact refer to the playing area may best be seen by an aerial view.

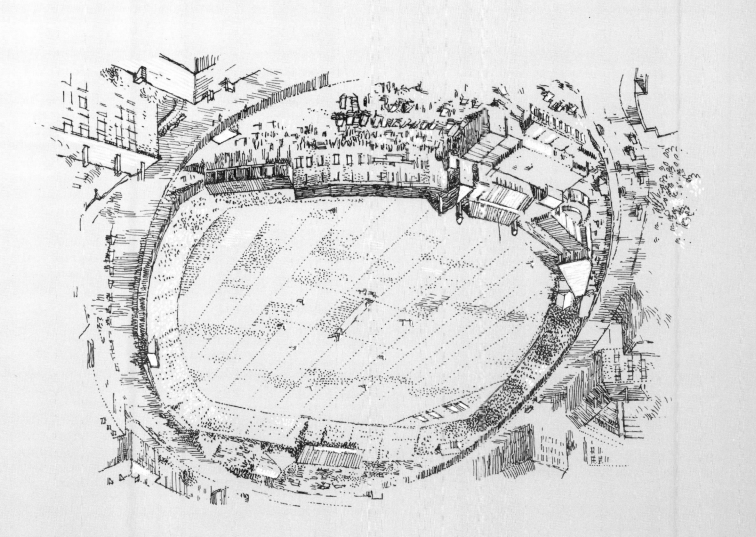

vided for them and thus they would gravitate to the beer tent. Even changing-rooms were reserved for the amateurs, so it was not unusual for the professionals to arrive at Lord's ready for play. Everybody knows of the segregation when the two sorts walked on to the field through different gates.

Though it is on the one hand easy to state that superficially one cricket ground is like any other, more demanding is the task of deciding what comprise the essential facets of any example. In other words, is there a model?

The answer to such a question must surely be that there are certain structures and features which any ground worthy of first-class cricket must possess. How they are arranged and what their character is creates that quality we call individuality. Add the historical associations and the environs, and you have the *genius loci*—the spirit of the place.

For most grounds the principal building is the pavilion. Its style may be homely, half timbered or imposingly classical, but whatever the architect's choice, it must satisfy the needs of two groups of users. For the players the dressing-rooms come first: not located at the back, with no view of the play, but having a balcony or at least generous windows on to the field; yet there should also be privacy and a certain distancing from the public gaze. The emergence of a team or batsman should

be gladiatorial: from the mystery of the pavilion the heroes enter the arena. For the Members the shelter and comfort are equally important, but more is required—a Long Room where the memorabilia, the photographs, the trophies can be tangible evidence of the club's collective memory. Both groups will want the pavilion to be 'looking down the wicket' and thereby is the problem, for the pitch should run north to south, and the batsman will certainly expect to have sightscreens. Where then should the pavilion be? If it is on the north side it will have little shade for the members, if on the south no sun. Unhappy is the wicket that runs east-west, for the evening sun and the looming shadows are the bane of every man on the field. Is the better solution to have the pavilion parallel to the pitch, as at Old Trafford or Cardiff? One thing is certain, any compromise between these is unhappy: the worst of both worlds.

After the pavilion, the scoreboard; for if the former bears the clock, the latter makes the time significant. Hierarchy now enters, with the 'main' scoreboard positioned so that those in the pavilion can easily see it, and its lesser brother usually beside the pavilion itself. Here comes another problem. Should the scorers be near the main scoreboard, or in communication only by ground telephone or, as has been known, by waving handkerchief? Nowadays the captains demand statistics like over-rates or scoring-pace, yet so often the scorers are tucked away in some 'cubby-hole' accessible only by those with a head for heights or a sound heart—at Lord's for example there are seventy-five steps to climb, and in the 1840s provision there was merely a platform eight feet above the ground without protection from the weather. And who cares if the scorers have to walk right across the ground at the intervals, yet be up-to-date in their records and back in their seats for the first ball of resumed play?

On some grounds there is a close association between the scorebox and the press box. It is not infrequently the case that reporters and journalists share the same exposure to the elements; sometimes they have even harsher conditions. To have a clear view of the scoreboard as well as the pitch, to be able to communicate quickly and easily with scorers, to have a telephone available may not seem excessive demands, but our model ground may not mirror reality. And what of the radio or television commentators: those rickety-looking scaffolds supporting a tarpaulin or shed perhaps represent the more useful accommodation for they are at least looking down the pitch, but pity the commentator who is able to have this view only through a monitor. It is worth observing that the television picture tends to present a very distorted impression of a ground, not only in proportion and scale but also in omitting, by its cameras' location, the chief visual feature, the pavilion. When pavilion is parallel to pitch there is a more faithful composition.

However we are concerned with spectators at the ground rather than those at home, for it is they who are the life-blood of the game. Advertisement boards around the boundary, and sponsors' boxes in their favoured stands may represent the much-needed financial support, but it is the crowd that gives humanity and occasion. Not that the spectators have always been welcome, indeed it is said that admission was first levied in an effort to keep them out. As we have noted, seating at Lord's was very spartan in the 1830s. But inexorably needs were recognised: the local inn would despatch a pot-boy round the ground, stands began to be provided, beer and refreshment tents appeared, and in some welcome instances a band to play. Today is it only Canterbury, Chesterfield and Scarborough which perpetuate this delightful practice?

The crowd, as much as the ground, has its character. Many a player has had good reason to remember his performance by the comments of varying discernment which float across the field. To try to decide on the ideal size of crowd is impossible; but there is no doubt that under 5,000 must be considered a poor attendance, and for a Test Match no crowd can be too large. That electric charge of match atmosphere owes its generation to the spectators, transforming a mediocre side, coaxing the

diffident, challenging the showman.

Yet every player is dependent on the ground, and that means the groundsman. Obviously such factors as the light, the trees, the reflection of sun on car windscreen, the wind, dust, sea-mist, pollen, even greenfly, wasp, bee or other insect can, and do, affect a performance, often unnoticed by the spectator. But the surface of uncertain level, such as is found near the touchline of a football pitch, or a previous block-hole, can turn a superb piece of fielding into an inept display. In early years the preparation of a pitch was managed by sheep: at Lord's there was no groundsman till 1864, and the introduction of a mowing machine strongly resisted.

Thus our model ground will have adequate provision for all that equipment—brushes, pails, rollers, mower, covers—which appear each in due time during a match, and make their contribution to the richness of activity.

And surely, somewhere on the ground there will be an indoor school. Perhaps it will serve double-duty as a dining-room, but in the winter it reverberates to the sound of bats. I like to think that the first indoor school

The ground at Cheltenham College presents a scene that contrasts with the great metropolitan arenas, yet these more modest settings have had quite as dramatic events. Here for example in 1893 the Gloucestershire wicket-keeper stumped consecutively three Somerset batsmen, to perform the only such hat-trick in first-class cricket.

was that of John Willes who in 1807 used his Kentish barn to develop his round-arm bowling. However, his practising was scantily rewarded, for in the M.C.C. v Kent match at Lord's in 1822 he was no-balled, and throwing down the ball—who says that tantrums are a modern occurrence?—left the ground, never to again play in a first-class match.

Yet there has been change since then: the character of play, the behaviour of players, the 'razmataz' of supporters, the sleeveless shirt, the protective helmet—the successor of the towel that Daft wore when he went in to bat after G. Summers had received a fatal blow on the head from Platt at Lord's in 1870—the dangling medallion, the congratulatory hugs, the innovations of limited run-up, or leg-side fielder, the list could go on.

Of course grounds are changing too. Pressures are mounting to give more prominence to advertising, to encourage other uses sporting and social, to introduce shops and funfairs, cinemas, restaurants, and to use them all the year round. Inevitably there are many who would regret this, but unless money comes from other sources, the choice is already determined.

Nevertheless, the essence of a cricket ground will not easily be destroyed. There will still be that sparkle of white wood, that sudden hush as the bowler delivers, that beauty of blue sky after rain, the immemorial trees, the tents and flags, the smell of grass, the measured pace of the match.

Grounds are part of the health of the game, and 'going to the cricket' an indivisible component of its continuance.

Derbyshire

County Ground, Nottingham Road, Derby DE2 6DA

THE COUNTY club was formed in 1870, and from 1873 when the category of first-class sides became established it was included. However, in 1887 it alone amongst all the counties now considered first-class was unable to sustain that designation, not regaining the status till 1895.

In the 1880 season Derbyshire played five matches including one against the Australia Touring side, and they all took place at Derby.

However fifty years later a very different pattern is seen. Fifteen home matches were played, only six at Derby. Five were at Chesterfield which had the Austra-lians match that year; Ilkeston had two, while Burton-on-Trent and Buxton each had one.

In 1980 Chesterfield again had the Tourists, this time the West Indies, and the same number of County Championship fixtures. Derby was given only four, Burton, Buxton and Ilkeston one apiece.

The county colours are chocolate, amber and light blue.

The emblem is the rose and crown, echoing the county coat of arms which has a red and gold tudor rose.

DERBY

IT SAYS much for the variety as well as individuality of first-class cricket grounds that the first in county order should owe its character to another sport. For the county ground of Derbyshire on the north-east side of the city has been known as the racecourse for over a century. The traffic which sweeps round the vast roundabout, called strangely the Pentagon, on its way to Nottingham may catch a glimpse of the grandstand and believe that horseboxes or racegoers may debouch on to the A52. But the jockeys, the trainers, bookies and all the particular paraphernalia have gone. Yet something of the atmosphere of a race meeting persists: certainly the wide vista

is still there; the Edwardian grandstand still has its viewing dome, used by Royalty; heavy neo-classical columns and consoles echo the imperial carving of the rose and crown and the date 1911; the red brick hotel; the jockeys' quarters half-timbered Tudor gables, rustic porches, end in a veritable signal box; there is a paddock area, though on the south side the stables have gone, boasting to the east a tea bar that has itself been superseded by the hockey club and the football club.

Much else has changed. The back of the grandstand is used as Ministry of Agriculture offices, and it is to be hoped that the favoured windows on the west side are allocated to cricket-loving civil servants on match days. Fortunately the Grandstand Hotel still exists as such though it is no longer residential. The committee and sponsors have the 'signal box', and everybody looks across to the scoreboard away to the west. Next to it awkwardly aligned, an indication of the way the square has moved, sits the concrete stand of former years. The players and the secretary's staff have taken over from the jockeys, while the members' enclosure has its fencing and white screens to give some protection from the wind that comes sweeping from the south-west.

But what a fine view there is of the city beyond. The

The grandstand with its viewing dome.

tall light-standards of the Pentagon are echoed by the magnificent tower of Derby Cathedral; away to the south over the railway line, domes, spires and blocks of offices or flats repeat the perpendicular. While the edge of the ground is emphasised and softened by a line of trees planted in 1973—a scheme that was the joint effort of the Civic Society, the Derby County Football Club and the Trent Motor Traction Co. (a delightfully Edwardian title). It is to be hoped the trees do not suffer in the same way as those on the north side of the ground, whose permanent lean shows more eloquently than anything else just how penetrating the wind can be.

But it is not a desolate ground. There is activity throughout the year in the indoor school by the entrance gates. The five hockey pitches, the two football pitches as well as the five cricket squares are well-used by local amateur clubs, indeed international hockey has been played here.

When the County XI matches are held, then the marquees appear, forms and canvas chairs range around the boundary, caravans and cars fill the paddock, yet so spacious is the place that a gate of 10,000 would not appear crowded.

What Derby lacks of course is a pavilion. Maybe one day the city council, who own the ground, will see their way to providing one, not only as a better focus for the players but also as a place where the history of the club can be expressed. For there is much that is worth remembering.

It was on this ground in 1868 that the South Derbyshire C.C., predecessor of the county club, met the Australian Aborigines, the first Touring side, and defeated them by 139 runs. Great feats of bowling in that match included four wickets in four balls by John Smith of Clifton near Ashbourne. A photograph of the winning team has survived, indeed it may well be the oldest we have. The association with Australia in those early years persisted, for it was to the Racecourse Ground that Spofforth the 'demon bowler' came when he played for the county—he married a girl from Breadsall.

In 1898 Derbyshire scored 645 against Hampshire; in 1902 it was Warwickshire that saw the home side make 561. But Kent showed that visitors could also make large scores here when in 1908 the southern county amassed 615. In 1914 Derbyshire in its match with Essex could produce only 31, and against Somerset in 1935 but four more. Of the batsmen associated with this ground the name Storer must merit high place, for in 1896 W. Storer took a century in each innings off the Yorkshire bowling, being the first professional cricketer to achieve this, while H. Storer found the Essex attack more to his liking, scoring 209 in 1929, incidentally participating in a record first wicket stand of 322 with

J. Bowden, and four years later increasing his success to 232. Another prolific innings on this ground was seen in the match against Sussex in 1937 when T. S. Worthington ended with 238 not out.

The Racecourse wicket has tended to be slow, and the frequently arctic conditions cannot have helped the numb fingers of the bowlers. Nevertheless W. H. Copson in the 1937 game with Warwickshire captured in thirteen balls no less than six wickets, four of which were in as many successive deliveries. Some twenty-one years later against Sussex F. C. Brailsford took a wicket with his first ball in the game.

CHESTERFIELD

HERE is no windswept bracing racecourse as at Derby, but luxuriant mature trees, set in a park. The flower beds are as colourful as one could wish; the lake nearby has ducks whose cries can sometimes be so appropriate at the fall of a wicket, indeed the story is too good to dismiss that when Laurie Johnson 'bagged a pair' in the Sussex match two ducks from the lake walked off with him.

For the cricket ground at Chesterfield is set in Queen's Park, one of those commemorating Victoria's Jubilee. So as might be expected the circular field has all the domesticity of the nineteenth century. There is a bandstand where happily a week-end match will enjoy the musical background; a delightful conservatory worthy of Joseph Paxton himself stands sufficiently far away to be secure from towering sixes; and at the town or lake end a miniature railway has taken away the possibility of a similar hit landing, as in the past, on a wagon. Now a graceful bridge links the park with the town whose brick town hall still succeeds in being visible on the skyline despite new tower blocks. But above all of course, the eye fastens on the famous—though not unique, Barnstaple would insist—twisted spire of the church of All Saints, and its being 238 feet high ensures that the trees do not compete with it.

It is a family ground, even the pavilion is on an intimate scale, while the press box is surely a garden shed. Yet all this, far from detracting from the quality of the

The view from the dome above the racecourse grandstand on the left are the former jockeys' quarters, while beyond the field to the west rise the towers and spires of Derby with the cathedral most prominent.

Chesterfield's fine ground in Queen's Park has the famous crooked spire rising behind the trees. [following pages]

game, seems to add a charm as well as an air of informality. Like as not you will see shoppers making their way home, or hear the excited cries of children boating on the lake. It is unlikely you will see more than 8,000 spectators though; the temporary seats will not spoil your enjoyment of the setting; and if you have a mind you may even leave the park bench and join the regulars who recline on the grassy bank—what better way is there to watch cricket at Chesterfield?

It is a small ground, slow to dry, often providing a quick green wicket. So it is hardly surprising that matches here have proved to be high—or very low—scoring. In 1900, for instance Essex made 597 in six hours, then on the final day found themselves shot out for 97. Revenge came for Derbyshire in 1928 when 552 must have been much to their liking. Then in 1957 Gladwin and Jackson humbled Middlesex in their second innings with 13 for 9.

The name of Graveney has represented the southern county of Gloucestershire on this ground: in 1949 J. K. R. took 10 Derbyshire wickets for 66, and five years later T. W. made 222.

An unusual occurrence took place in 1946 when the Yorkshire bowlers Bowes and Smailes unaccountably had problems of length and pace, till Hutton at third man suggested the pitch be checked. The groundsman's face must have been red when it was found to be 24 yards. But perhaps it was the partnership of Brown and Tunnicliffe here which most thrills all followers of Yorkshire, for to score 554 on any ground must rank as something of an achievement; to do it in so pleasant a setting must have made the journey well worthwhile in 1898. That journey, from whatever county, is as rewarding today when it ends at Chesterfield.

But of course Derbyshire offers other journeys in search of cricket. There is Burton-on-Trent, or Trent College; and maybe once again Buxton and Ilkeston will see their grounds used by the county side.

Essex

County Ground, New Writtle Street, Chelmsford, CM2 0RW

FORMED in 1876, the club had to wait till 1895 before achieving the status of first-class. Although the County Cricket Council of 1887 recognised its existence, together with many counties like Durham, Cheshire and Norfolk that have never become contestants in the Championship, the ill-fated council of 1890 designated it second-class.

A century ago there were inevitably no Championship home fixtures for Essex, but fifty years ago fourteen were arranged, and moreover the Australian Tourists came. Leyton was then the predominant ground with nine matches; Chelmsford, Colchester and Southend had two each.

In 1980 the fixture list showed eleven Championship fixtures, five at Chelmsford, two at Colchester, Southend and Ilford, but unhappily no Tourist match.

Club colours are blue, gold and red.

The county emblem consists of three seaxes, the notched scimitars used as a device by the East and Middle Saxons, and to avoid confusion with the other county Middlesex which has the same weapons, the word Essex is displayed.

CHELMSFORD

MANY county clubs have made it their practice to play home matches on a large number of grounds, but in the case of Essex it was followed to the extreme by having no county ground as such, rather the games took place at various centres with the equipment necessary for cricket travelling there also. So, from 1933, Chelmsford was

---

The mobile scoreboard is seen at Chelmsford's County Ground, in the distance, the classical façade of the Shire Hall, the cathedral spire, and on the extreme left the pavilion. [following pages]

but one of those eight or nine grounds.

However since 30th March 1965 Essex has had a home, and Chelmsford was the county ground at last. It is a pleasant place, beside the River Can. Indeed it is not unknown for parsimonious spectators to do their viewing from the farther bank. Certainly the Upper-deck passengers of the buses travelling over the nearby bridge have a few seconds of free cricket, though for how many more years is debatable since the club has planted conifers, and intends to erect a permanent scoreboard in front. You may well wonder why no scoreboard exists as there have been county fixtures here from 1926—and incidentally the first was against Somerset, ending in an exciting if frustrating tie with the last Essex batsman dashing to the wicket only to see the umpire remove the bails. But at least till 1979 the famous mobile scoreboard still made its peregrinations, and Chelmsford was no exception.

Let us hope that those conifers will not grow so tall as to hide the pedimented Shire Hall, for it was there in 1876 that the club was formed. Another feature in partial eclipse is the cathedral whose green copper spire defiantly rises above the new tower-blocks of commerce.

On the east side of the ground the grey brick hospital provides for, we hope, patient watching; as, in return, the field serves as a helicopter landing pad for urgent cases—there is a gate behind the mobile scoreboard for quick access.

In its early years the club leased Leyton ground, then rural in its character, and something of that aspect persists here in Chelmsford, for you may approach it by a narrow road and find yourself between tents and trees.

Inevitably change is taking place. The pavilion dates from 1970, pleasingly softened by wood weatherboarding. Its balcony unfortunately is square to the wicket, perhaps in an unconscious desire to savour the pace of J. Lever, or maybe recall K. Farnes of pre-war days. Certainly it would not have been to concentrate on the latter's batting technique, for it is remembered with amusement that in the 1936 match with Derbyshire, Farnes was dropped no less than five times in one over, though in fairness it must be added that he was eventually caught, to give the visitors victory. In compensation, the 1979 match against Kent showed the home batsmen in such form that in the course of the morning's play eight sixes were lofted into neighbouring gardens, resulting in the loss of four balls. The consequence of this display of belligerence was a search party during the lunch interval; its thoroughness was such that not four, but five, balls were retrieved.

The magnificent performance by the club in winning the County Championship after 103 years will surely result in the secretary's office attracting more of those plaques, pennants and other mementoes which help to record a club's history.

Eight years after the pavilion's building, its neighbour has come into full use. Nowhere better does the changing patronage of cricket show itself than in the private box and 'executive suite'. For this is a club within the club, having facilities for functions in wintertime, and limiting its membership to 250. The ground floor sponsors' boxes hold fifty each; there is a committee room, and everything reflects the new standard of comfort and hospitality expected by these supporters. Yet it is reassuring to find the mayor's tent still there with its geraniums fronting it, and—a homely touch—the flagpole in an oil drum.

It is a small ground, perhaps the smallest county ground in the country, and you are aware of this particularly because of the noise of traffic both road and rail. Inevitably it is not perfect, there is a slope from east to west, and the proximity of the river brings its own problems, as well as advantages, as the banking in front of the hospital indicates. However it is but five minutes from the railway station, there is easy access from the town, and the facilities are good.

Confidence in the club's future is well expressed in the indoor school that stands behind the pavilion. It was opened in 1977 to provide coaching for boys—and girls—as well as for use by other clubs. Already it has admirably met this obligation.

The future then for the county cricket ground at New Writtle Street, Chelmsford looks promising: the crowds are lively, the players are adventurous. And as if to echo this, the paintwork in the pavilion is sparkling and fresh—even if it is bright orange, with red, orange and blue lights! How well a club's cricket is shown in its ground.

There has been a price paid, perhaps. Chelmsford's gain must be at the expense of those other grounds once visited by the club: Southend, Colchester—where A. E. Fagg of Kent made those unique two double-centuries in one match—and Ilford survive, but what of Brentwood, Romford, Clacton, Leyton or Westcliff? All one can say is that it is good to see such a long struggle rewarded and in a sense applaud a club come into its own.

Glamorgan

6 High Street, Cardiff CF1 2PW

ALTHOUGH the club dates from 1888, it did not appear amongst the first-class counties till 1921 being the last to do so. However, in the 1890 Council it was designated as a third-class county, and it was doubtless with some satisfaction that, together with Northamptonshire, it emerged to represent one of the two twentieth-century newcomers to the Championship. That it also stood for the Principality's cricketing coming-of-age must have meant much beyond Offa's Dyke.

In 1930 the season saw Cardiff—in those days Arms Park—and Swansea as the chief grounds, six matches at the former, seven including the Australia match at the latter; with Pontypridd having one game. In 1980, the balance between the two cities was finer: six each though Swansea again had the Tourists.

Being in a sense a national club it is possible for a home match to be played many miles away, at for example Colwyn Bay or Aberystwyth, while nearer grounds can well be 'away'!

Club colours are blue and gold; the predictable emblem a daffodil. Interestingly the old Glamorgan had no evidence of the national flower in its coat of arms.

CARDIFF

IN ONE sense, as already suggested, the whole of Wales is Glamorgan's, for when playing at Colwyn Bay or Aberystwyth these must surely be home matches. In another sense Glamorgan is never at home, as it has no county ground and its administrative headquarters are on the first floor of a building in Cardiff's busy High Street.

Nevertheless Cardiff's Sophia Gardens, despite being owned by the Corporation, leased to the athletic club and sub-let to the Glamorgan County Cricket Club, since the disappearance of Cardiff Arms Park from the fixture list, must be thought of as the county ground. It is part of a fast-developing national sports centre, dominated by the vast dark brown bulk of that building.

The pavilion dates from 1969, the time of the move from Arms Park. It is dwarfed by the sports centre behind, and yet through its multi-angled roof façade manages to assert some identity. Certainly it is well equipped with six changing-rooms, dining-room and bar; but all this is as much for the cricket, tennis and rugby players of Cardiff Athletic Club as for the county club. Indeed when Glamorgan plays here you will first have to find a blue-and-yellow caravan if you wish to see the secretary. In the pavilion you will not see photographs of the county teams, for they are at 6 High Street. So inevitably something is lacking so far as a sense of history is concerned.

However, there is always some evidence of the past to be found, even in the new grounds, and at Sophia Gardens it is the buildings on the east side. Their weather-boarding and triangular-ended fencing are reminders of Arms Park, for that is where they used to be. Even the spartan backed seats have the air of earnest Welsh supporters, with but a sun awning as a concession to the old score box.

The pitch is parallel to the pavilion which means that sightscreens are possible each end. It has a quick drying soil, thanks to the underlying gravel, and flooding is no danger, though the river does cause some movement of the sub-soil. The wicket can be challenging in its uneven bounce, for it needs marl to tame its speed.

On the north-west is the fine scoreboard, largely the gift of Sir Edward Lewis, and beyond can be seen the tennis courts, the rugby pitches, and then the mature trees that add so much to the attractiveness of the ground. But it must not be thought that the club has made no contribution in the relatively short time it has used the field. In front of the concrete terracing each side of the pavilion you will see rose bushes, and you will note a number of young trees too. These owe their presence here to Wilfred Wooller, sometime captain and later secretary of the club.

The seating around the ground is temporary, with a capacity of perhaps 11,000. It is hoped in the future to build administrative offices for the club at the Cathedral Road end, and when that is realised, the television cameras and radio commentators will be spared a daunting climb to the top of the scaffold!

Sponsors have their own tent to bring a festival atmosphere to the place, enhanced by the three flag poles

Sophia Gardens, Cardiff showing to the south the vast sports centre and, nearer, the older parts of the cricket ground building. [following pages]

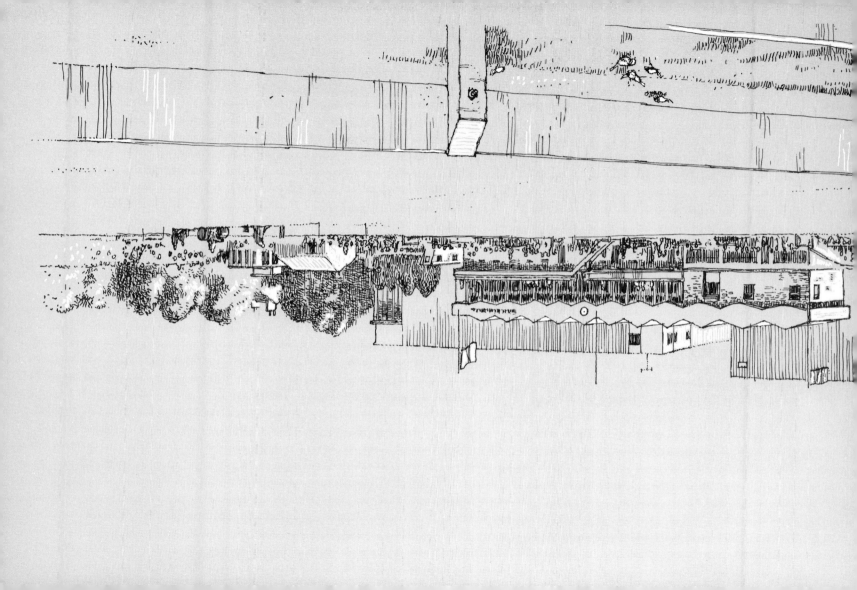

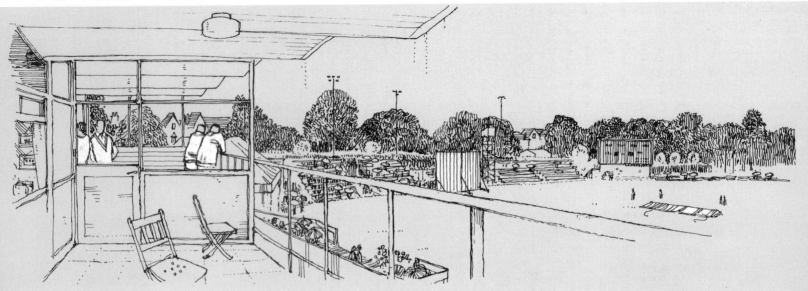

on the pavilion which fly, on the centre, the athletic club's colours, on the east or left the visitor's, and on the west the home team's flag. It can indeed be a colourful scene, for the famous green grass of Wales sets off the dark conifers, the bright roses and the sombre ribbing of the sports centre—even when it is raining.

Looking westwards from the pavilion at Sophia Gardens, Cardiff.

A decade or so is not long to build up a store of records for this ground, and one wishes it were permissible to transfer the memories from Arms Park, not least that of 1951 when Glamorgan scored 587 for 8 off Derbyshire, or of 1934 when G. Lavis and C. Smart put on 263 for the fourth wicket. But we must content ourselves with M. J. Khan's 114 not out before lunch in the 1969 match against Worcestershire.

SWANSEA

IT IS called St Helen's ground and for character as well as situation it is one of the memorable places for every county cricketer.

For one thing it is by the sea, not just near it, but almost on it. From the pavilion terracing there is a superb view, over the field, to the ships, whether ore carriers making their way to Port Talbot, or oil tankers going into Swansea; and from the scoreboard terraces it is an easy matter to keep surveillance of the family on the sands.

In the past there was the added diversion of watching the oldest passenger line just outside the gates. I mean of course the famous Mumbles railway. It is worth digressing, before concerning ourselves with the ground, to say a little more about this line. There is something reminiscent of those whimsical trains drawn by Rowland Emett, in the Oystermouth and Mumbles line. From 1804 to 1896 it was horse-drawn, from 1877 to 1929 horse power alternated with steam, with electricity taking over in 1929 with the largest tram in the world. It was a single track, passing places being provided at intervals, one outside the ground. But on 5th January 1960 all this came to an end, though it is hoped to revive horse-drawn services on the west part.

Add to this a prospect of the Mumbles lighthouse and lifeboat, with Devon cliffs in the far distance, and you have a seat offering pretty well everything needful for a day's cricket.

From this place by the scoreboard the vast rugby stand reminds you that this is a shared ground. Indeed it must be the only instance of the two games actually overlapping to the extent of a third of the cricket square. It is a big ground too: four acres of it, and a third of a mile round its boundary. No wonder batsmen consider this to have the longest walk to the wicket, and indeed the steepest climb back, since there are over seventy steps to the pavilion. Even the pavilion has a seaside air about it, with white walls capped by four bright-green tile corner turrets, like a toy fort, complete with public announcement trumpets to frighten would-be attackers.

Behind the pavilion rise on Brynmill grey tiers of terraced houses, steep gabled and worthy of Dylan Thomas, until the skyline leads the eye eastwards to find its focus on the radio-mast-topped Kilvey Hill. Nearer at hand stand the unmistakable stone tower of Swansea's Guildhall, built in the best traditions of Wembley Stadium.

The view of St Helen's, Swansea, from the Rugby Stand has the Guildhall tower, Kilvey Hill rising behind it, and leading round to the north the terraces of Brynmill. [following pages]

Two more intriguing buildings repay attention before we look at the ground itself. Just behind the scoreboard, now half-hidden by trees stands the Madame Patti pavilion. It was her 'winter gardens' at Craig-y-Nos near Dan yr Ogoff, but in 1920 it was re-erected here in Victoria Park. How much it reflects the Edwardian age, a time when cricket recognition had not yet been given to Glamorgan. However, not far away, near the memorial gates to the ground, you will see the Cricketers Hotel, that displays all the confidence of the last century. Elaborate balcony decoration of cast iron, sturdy window surrounds, motifs of bat, ball and stumps proclaim to the world that here is a real cricket ground.

The great rugby stand which dates from the 1920s has a dignity that sums up the game's rich history in South Wales. There are gothic doors and windows, while an overhang outside gives protection to the countless votaries at this shrine.

The pavilion frankly is disappointing, for it has little atmosphere of cricket. Indeed, even though it is part of the Swansea clubhouse must rugby photos, shields and caps predominate? The verandah which might have helped to give character has gone, and the steep concrete

From the pavilion at St Helen's the sea does not seem far away; to the lone batsmen the pitch must appear rather more distant.

terracing precludes the deck chairs that were so much a feature of past years. The new dressing-rooms below the dining-room are an undoubted improvement, but it needs much more to give St Helen's the pavilion it deserves.

The field has a slight slope to the west, and its quick-drying property owes much to the fact that the 18 inches of soil lies on sand, sand which comes readily to the surface on the paths behind the scoreboard. Another feature of most seaside grounds is present here at Swansea, namely the mists or fog that can rapidly transform a sunny scene into a ghostlike fiasco. Perhaps it also happens when other activities take place on the field, like Rugby League Internationals, the odd soccer match, hockey training, jazz festival, and even 'It's a Knockout'. Such is St Helen's versatility that its dominating 140-foot floodlight pylon has a part to play in these.

Memories are rich and varied at Swansea. The oldest spectators will still talk of Glamorgan's 36 against Hampshire in 1922; of Sussex making 75 in the first innings and 356 in the second in 1928; of A. H. Dyson scoring a century before lunch off Kent on the first day of the 1937 season; of J. Hills and J. C. Clay putting on an undefeated 203 for the ninth wicket against Worcestershire in 1929. Many a young member will have stored for future use the 544 for 4 scored by the West Indies in 1976, and wish he had been alive to have seen M. J. Turnbull dominate the Worcestershire attack in 1937 to the tune of 233—200 coming in 188 minutes. For M. J. Khan this ground was as memorable as Cardiff's, for here in 1967 he scored 147 of Pakistan's runs before lunch; for C. H. Loyd nine years later, 120 minutes were enough to give him 201 not out for the West Indies.

Bowlers have also enjoyed success here. In 1937 J. C. Clay took 17 of Worcestershire's wickets for 212 runs, in 1965 J. S. Pressdee returned figures of 9 for 43 against Yorkshire; and 1925 saw V. W. C. Jupp for Northants enjoy the match analysis of 15 for 52. But two matches stand out: that in 1972 against Northamptonshire again, when the Glamorgan openers R. Fredericks and A. Jones put on 330 for the first wicket, and the celebrated over by G. Sobers in 1968 when the thirty-six 'barrier' was broken with six successive sixes off the home team's M. Nash.

Gloucestershire

Phoenix County Ground, Nevil Road, Bristol BS7 9EJ

THE CLUB was formed in 1871 and almost immediately took its place amongst the eight leading teams of the country. Thus its designation as a first-class county dates from the seminal 1873.

A century ago there were but five Championship games in the county: three at Clifton College, Bristol, where also the Australians played that year, and two at Cheltenham College. Fifty years later in 1930 Clifton had two, Cheltenham four, and the Wagon Works ground at Gloucester three.

The remaining six, including the Tourist match, were at Ashley Down, Bristol—the present county ground.

Fifty years on again and the Home Championship matches are now seven at Bristol, three at Cheltenham, one at Gloucester, and the Tourists still at the headquarters.

Club colours are rich and varied: blue, gold, brown, sky-blue, green and red.

The emblem also boasts a complexity, being based on the 1569 coat of arms of the City of Bristol. However the observant may identify subtle changes within the shield where for example the ship emerging from the castle now has all visible sails unfurled. More obvious are the substitution of lions for the unicorns as supporters, and the helmet for those entwined arms bearing scales and snake.

BRISTOL

THERE can be little doubt that you are approaching a cricket ground at Ashley Down on the northern side of Bristol, for the roads bear the names of the first-class counties, the minor counties and the two universities.

If you are still uncertain then the entrance gates should

The pavilion at Bristol with its more recent extensions.

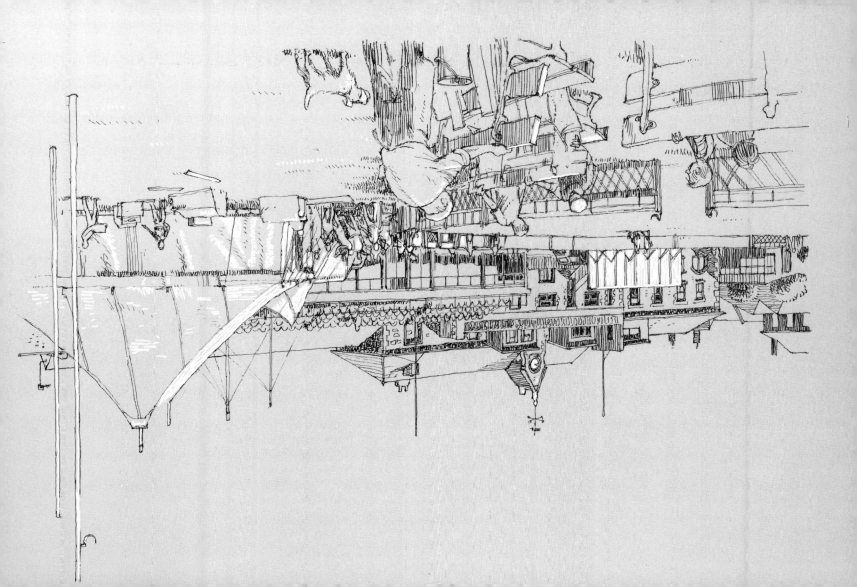

set your mind at rest, for there on one of the massive piers facing you is a 1948 plaque bearing a majestic but familiar figure, that of W. G. Grace.

He is in the stance made famous by the artist Stuart Wortley in his painting of 1890, and his presence here is appropriate, for the great Gloucestershire batsman initiated this ground, even if when he led the county club it used that at Clifton College. Since 1976 the Phoenix Assurance Company has owned the ground and its development as a sports centre seems bright. Already there are facilities for squash, tennis and even golf—in the form of a winter driving range.

The ground has had an interesting history of ownership, a history of financial difficulties ending in timely rescues. The first instance was in 1915—hardly an encouraging year for cricket anyway—when the club found itself so much in debt that at a special general meeting the previous October it had been decided that no fixtures should be arranged for the next year and that the professionals on the playing staff would receive no payment, a move to allow them freedom to qualify for other counties. However, it was the firm of J. S. Fry which brought respite by purchasing the ground, thus giving it the new name 'Fry's'. By sad coincidence, 1915 was the very year W. G. Grace died at Eltham in Kent.

By 1932 the club was strong enough to buy back the ground, and thus it continued, with the inevitable interruption of World War II when the Royal Navy, Army and the United States forces took it over. Now the rising Phoenix representing a further ready helper takes its place on the wall beyond the Grace gate pier.

But there are other benefactors too. The garden seats, each with a nameplate commemorating one of Gloucestershire's players, are a delightful acquisition—and a hundred of them were given by another firm having Bristol associations: Imperial Tobacco.

It is a ground with much character. There is a feeling of being on top of the world, without the accompanying bleakness. To the north-west the panorama of a great city suggests itself while around the boundary all the buildings are low. The predominant colour, grey, can be seen in them as in the pavilion, and somehow it gives a richness and maturity to the scene.

There are trees to provide just the right touch of green; and the boundary trellis fencing is echoed by the park-type benches. Maybe the rambler roses and the

Hardly a cricket scene, yet the golf driving range plays an important part in the activity at Bristol.

The Orphanage end at Bristol with the Jessop Tavern in front has a spaciousness of sky rarely found in a city. [following pages]

strawberries and ice-cream stall have gone, but there are still some marquees to grace the pavilion on Lancashire Road end.

The pavilion has suffered change too. In 1976 the balcony had to go, as had its verandah, but fortunately the cast iron decoration was saved. Some criticism has been levelled at the lack of dignity in the façade, and admittedly the clock turret, off-centre, is a little insignificant. But there is a homely solidity about the building in keeping with the age.   At the opposite end of the field stands the long low silhouette of what was Mullers Orphanage.

This was the scheme instigated by the Prussian clergyman George Muller, and the first block of 1847, like a workhouse, was for 300 children. The other buildings followed in 1857, 1862, 1868 and 1870 so that eventually over 7,000 children were housed—if that be the right term—in this enterprise.

Today it is part of Bristol Polytechnic and Brunel Technical College. The restrained rhythm of windows is continued in the buildings to the east side of the ground, behind the 1958 Jessop Tavern and the main scoreboard of 1971 and behind the mound stand of 1960 where, in the winter, golfers practise, from 10 a.m. to 9 p.m., their drives to targets dotted over the field.

Next to the pavilion is the Hammond Room, of 1977, and I wonder how many visitors assume it refers to 'Wally'. But in fact it is in memory of Cyril, one of the promotion chiefs so necessary nowadays. Perhaps there will be a room for 'W.R.' at Bristol in due course, for few deserve it more. As an all-round cricketer he was underrated, an opening bowler able to return an analysis of 9 for 23 before lunch on the first day, and then score 80 in the afternoon. To his name stand 167 centuries, and two centuries in a match seven times. As has been well said, Hammond didn't walk to the wicket, he strode; and once there he surveyed the field with a patrician air looking not to see where the fielders were but where the boundaries offered themselves.

Well at least Jessop has his tavern, placed so appropriately at cover point. For here was another superlative fielder, to which must be added fast bowling and above all fast batting. He may not have the fastest innings or the fastest century; but he scored a century in less than 60 minutes six times, including 157 against a West Indies side, and, against Yorkshire, one in forty minutes. We must leave his immortal Test Match century in seventy-five minutes for the Oval.

And then there is W. G. Grace himself: he has a room, wood-panelled and rich in pictures. The famous hand is preserved in casting, the face peers from table 171737 (were there really that number made?), and the instantly recognisable figure stands nonchalantly between cricket ball ink-wells behind the pen-holder on the silver writing stand. What is there more to say about the 'Champion'? Gloucestershire-born of a Somersetshire doctor-father, his first memory was of a match at Stokes Croft Bristol when some of the players still wore top-hats; his best season 2,379 runs in 1871; his career topped 126 centuries, 54,896 runs and 2,876 wickets. But that was secondary to his achievement in almost half-a-century of transforming a pastime into a national game.

No other batsman in those days of rough pitches tamed the murderous fast bowler as he did; nobody else provided such a mixture of authority and boyish trick-ery; no-one but he could have interrupted a double century to win a hurdle championship; or throw a cricket ball 117 yards, or captain England at bowls, or raise the entrance fee when he was batting. But then there has only been one W. G.

Ashley Down's Phoenix ground deserves a Long Room, it deserves a gallery to display those pictures stored away in the pavilion attic—there must be, surely, some taken when the county achieved that remarkable tie with the 1930 Australian tourists here; or of Austra-lia's revenge in that invincible tour of 1948 when they settled for 774 for 7; or of T. W. Goddard's 17 for 106 in

The 'other' Grace Gates—at Ashley Down's Phoenix Ground, Bristol.

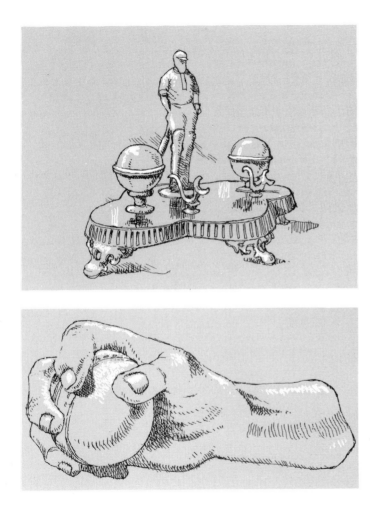

Memorabilia of the 'Champion' table and writing stand have perhaps less evocativeness than the cast of W. G.'s bowling hand.

one day against Kent in 1939, his 5 for 4 against Somerset in 1947; of Sadiq Mohammed's 163 not out and 150 in the 1976 Derbyshire match; of the 239 put on for the eighth wicket by Hammond and A. E. Wilson against Lancashire 1938—yes, much has happened here at Ashley Down.

CHELTENHAM

THE GREEN field, white tents, majestic chapel, school tower, and everywhere an air of tradition, leisure and echoes of Newbolt's *"Vitai Lampada"*—that surely is one unchanging concept of the perfect cricket ground. Cheltenham comes close to realising it. The county club has played here since 1872 when James Lillywhite (an appropriate enough name), cricket coach at Cheltenham College, suggested that during the summer holiday a fixture be here. It was typical of the enterprise of this Sussex man who founded *Wisden's* early rival, the *Cricketer's Companion* and it was also in keeping with the county club that he was given a free-hand together with £10 to arrange everything. Doubtless it flourished through the association of W. G. Grace who in the 1874 match against Surrey took 7 for 7 in the first innings, and 7 for 18 in the second; who in the 1876 match made

318 not out putting on 261 with W. Moberly for the fifth wicket. The 1877 match was against Nottinghamshire when Grace again distinguished himself by taking 17 wickets for 19 runs. It is interesting to note that whereas the visiting team comprised nine professionals and two amateurs, Gloucestershire's was ten amateurs and one-professional, W. Midwinter. He incidentally was the only player who took the field in Test Matches for both England and Australia. Not surprisingly that Notts match ended quickly, and, as promised on the posters, a game took place between Gloucestershire and Cheltenham. To balance the scales the county club used broomsticks instead of bats, yet E. M. Grace scored 104 and Midwinter 58 of the total 299.

By 1878 the fixture had another to follow, thus constituting a 'Cheltenham Week', for which Lillywhite was allocated £120.

Then in 1906 the addition of a third match elevated the Week to a Festival, which brought with it such 'fringe benefits' as a banquet at the 'Plough'.

Yes, it has been a ground where great things have happened. Even in that year 1906, the local 'Derby' could

---

The scene at Cheltenham College during the Cricket Festival has a timeless quality that nevertheless betrays evidence of change. [following pages]

not have been more spectacular with Worcestershire managing only 147 and 146 in reply to 523. Twenty-eight years later Sussex could not prevent the home side from scoring 608 for seven, and in the August of the following year one of Gloucestershire's moments of glory took place when the Tourists, South Africa, lost by 87 runs, W. R. Hammond making 123, and R. Sinfield 102, as well as taking 5 for 31. There was tragedy to follow for both D. A. C. Page the captain-elect and the South African captain, Cameron, were to die in a matter of months rather than years.

It is perhaps right that Cheltenham-born G. L. Jessop also be remembered at this ground. His particular contributions were to be epitomised in the 4 for 9 he achieved in 1895 against Yorkshire, and the fast batting in the second year of the Festival: 33 in thirteen minutes against Kent; 53 in fifteen minutes against Hampshire.

But we must not think of all the great things happening in the distant past. What of Zaheer Abbas who was undefeated with 205 and 108 in the 1977 match with Sussex? What of M. Procter's hat-trick of lbws in 1979 when Yorkshire experienced the same humbling as Essex had done seven years earlier at Westcliff?

Enough of these glories; the ground is attractive in its own right. Admittedly the chapel was not there when the Week started, but the twin-steepled gymnasium with its yellow brick and its trellised balcony was. Lilly-white saw the same fat-skirted spire of St Lukes to the north, while doubtless W. G. Grace had a professional appreciation of the general hospital portico erected the year he was born.

Some features remain even from the beginning of the Week: the canvas screening so delightfully ineffective in denying a free view; the challenging slope; the 'sentry box' on the balcony and the line of tents. One feature is new. The Eagle Star Administrative Head Office and Computer Centre towering behind the chapel has effectively changed that scene described at the start. Completed in 1968 this 200-feet high skyscraper despite its Bath stone facings has ensured that.

GLOUCESTER

FOR YEARS it was known as the Wagon Works ground, and certainly there is an austerity in its setting that reflects an engineer's cricket. But the Gloucester Railway Carriage and Wagon Company ground became the Gloucester Engineering Sports ground, and then the

At the Gloucester ground a new pavilion still has its old trees affording just a glimpse of the cathedral tower.

Winget, now it is to be Babcocks and Wilcox Sports ground. But it is the same firm as 150 years ago, and though buildings have been replaced, trees have grown and houses fill the neighbouring fields, I fancy those who made their way to the first county game here, in 1923 against Lancashire, would today feel at home. Robin's Wood Hill still rises to the east, and to the north the cathedral tower has not yet been entirely hidden by the semi's of Podsmead and Linden.

Some eight years ago there might have been a housing estate on the field, but the city council saved it from so inglorious a fate. On the other hand it did not quite succeed to the eminence of becoming the county ground, though that had been mooted.

It is undeniably a field that looks bleak when there is no county match. The buildings are few, and indeed some are very new. The pavilion was completed only in 1979 as part of an extensive redevelopment. Even the lounge, as it is called, looks about the same age, though in fact it started life as a fire brigade, or NFS, station in the Second World War, being built by the firemen themselves.

The scoreboard nevertheless is something of a museum-piece for it came from Bristol's Ashley Down ground, that is, Fry's ground, or the Phoenix ground—Gloucestershire seems to go in for changes of name. Ten plane trees line the pavilion boundary; a pity there was no 'twelfth' tree to take the place of the one that died, but perhaps in 1920 money was as tight as now. Certainly costs were lower, for the concrete wall on the city side of the ground was built for one shilling, or 5p, an hour.

The old clubhouse was a hospital in the last war, having, appropriately, been built as a First World War hospital and brought here.

Another building with a strange origin can be seen near the lounge, forming part of the bowling green's pavilion. The long dimension will suggest a railway carriage, and indeed closer inspection confirms it. For this was a product of the wagon works that in 1915 was ordered for the Argentine Railway. Unfortunately it completed only part of the voyage before the ship carrying it sank off Ushant. Eventually the carriage was salvaged and brought back to be the changing-room of the bowling club. But it has not completely forgotten its original purpose for the glass panes on the end doors still bear the monogram of the South American company.

On match days the ground takes on a very festive character, with tents lining the tennis court end—incidentally the tennis finished some ten years ago. There is the civic tent for the Mayor of Gloucester, the committee tent, the sponsors' tents, the scorers tent and the beer tent. The Press also has its tent on the other side of the scoreboard where there is a change in level, for once the ground sloped from south-east to north-west.

Beyond the terrace there is another cricket square, and indeed there are one football and three hockey pitches too. It must have been a considerable task levelling the surface; the interesting result is that the clay content of the soil rated at 236 pounds is the highest of any ground—Lord's is only 175, the Oval 160 and Hove 107. The consequence of this is that it breaks up very quickly.

Strange therefore that it is not spectacular bowling but high scores that are remembered here. (It was at the Spa ground in the city that Northamptonshire in 1907 managed only 12 runs; and where in 1882 W. H. Fowler hit a delivery from W. G. Grace 154 yards.) Perhaps it is fitting that the square was laid out by Arthur Paish who had played under Grace and Jessop.

In 1936 Gloucestershire made 485 against Nottinghamshire. It was T. Goddard's Benefit match, and what better way of marking it when Hammond contributed 317, his highest score in England? Hammond must have liked the ground for in the following season, against Leicestershire he and W. L. Neale made 321 together for the fourth wicket.

The 'Wagon Works' may not be Lord's—though nearby is the 'Oval', alas only tennis courts—but it has seen mighty scores and had some share in Gloucestershire's cricket history.

Hampshire

County Ground, Northlands Road, Southampton SO9 2TY

DESPITE the prominence given to Broad-Halfpenny Down in the literature of cricket—and it must be remembered that the Hambledon Club did not come into existence till six years after the game between Kent and All-England in 1744, the first of which a full record remains—Hampshire was not deemed a first-class county till 1895, thirty-two years after the club had been formed.

In the 1880 season but two home matches of Championship status were played: one at Bournemouth and the other at Southampton. However by 1930 Ports-mouth had joined them, and the resulting proportions were Portsmouth four, Bournemouth four, Southampton seven. In 1980 Basingstoke is added to the Championship list, Portsmouth has two games, Bournemouth and Southampton have four each.

Club colours are blue, gold and white.

It was in 1893 that the Club adopted the white Tudor rose as its emblem to go with the crown—strange, when it is remembered that the county has a red one. Perhaps it was chosen from those on the Southampton arms, for there have been both kinds there since 1575. Was it because here was a Yorkist town, and after all Yorkshire had some significance in cricket?

SOUTHAMPTON

THE COUNTY ground is some way from the docks and Southampton Water, being on the north side of the city, near to that wonderful asset, the Common. Surely no other comparable place has so fine an approach, and indeed as you drive down the Avenue it is not difficult to imagine this is still the Hampshire countryside, and that

The box-office is now a forgotten feature at Southampton.

the Cowherds Inn, just before you turn off to Northlands Road, is really on Broad Halfpenny Down.

It is a ground with as long a history as many for county cricket has been played here since 1885, yet curiously it has not accrued for itself the richness of memories its years deserve. One does not immediately think of Southampton when great matches, close finishes, or individual performances are recalled. True there was the 321 made by G. Brown and E. I. M. Barrett for the second wicket against Gloucestershire in 1920, and the 371 for 4 (for which C. G. Greenidge contributed 177) in the Gillette Cup match with Glamorgan in 1975. Yet such "swallows do not make a summer".

Perhaps the ground itself has not brought out the best in players. There is a strange lack of atmosphere, not unconnected maybe with the buildings. Two of them, the pavilion and the stand, are roughly equal in proportion, differentiated largely by the fact that the former has a cupola and dormer louvres, while the latter has more of a racecourse style. Both have assertive red tiles which together with the large amount of white paint give a certain stridency to the group. In 1965 these rather bland

Southampton's County Ground groups its buildings virtually in one part of the boundary. [following pages]

façades were joined by a further balcony, with a clock on the balustrade attempting to meet the need for some central focus.

The offices to the west have the air of a forlorn seaside villa of the modernistic school so popular in the inter-war years. But in fact this block—for that is what it may justly be termed—was opened in 1956. I recall the occasion when on that sunny morning H. S. Altham and P. Mead—by then sadly blind—performed the simple opening ceremony.

But without a doubt the interesting feature on this side of the ground is the gabled building that is sand-wiched between the offices and the pavilion, for it is the home team's dressing room and represents the last of the 1895 buildings.

Originally this ground was part of the Banister estate, a name perpetuated in the nearby road, and the stadium which lay at one time on the south side of the field. It was a source of some amusement to observe the patrons of the greyhound racing striving to enjoy both sports. Today a housing estate, and a 'Top-Rank' disco and conference centre take its place.

Housing, as flats, has appeared also on the east side of the ground, with all the prospects of broken windows from big hits, but thankfully a yard-arm is still visible nearby to give that nautical touch. Not that there is no other reminder of this being a seaport, for the bell that

hangs in front of the stand is from the Union-Castle ship *Athlone Castle* when she was broken-up in 1966.

It is unusual to find two commentary boxes, at opposite ends. Each on its scaffolding behind a sightscreen sends news of the match; that on the south to listeners to BBC Radio Solent; that on the north to less fortunate listeners in hospital.

There are interesting things to see here: the pavilion though lacking the impressiveness of many others has a rich collection of score cards, photographs, cigarette cards and cartoons by the local 'Oz', while behind the stand, now unused, remains the old ticket office complete with pigeon-hole.

And it is good to know that the civic centre's tower can still be seen, and indeed heard when the wind carries the carillon "O God our Help in Ages Past" across the city, even if the sirens of the *Queens* and *Normandie* are gone for ever.

BOURNEMOUTH

DEAN PARK, lies off the Lansdowne Road on the north

The view from inside the former professionals' pavilion.

side of the town and is encircled by Cavendish Road, names which leave little doubt of the aristocratic character of this ground. It is still privately owned, being part of the Cooper-Dean estate, and indeed very real evidence of the family's interest in the ground may be seen in the scoreboard, for, as the plaque records, it was given in 1974 by Miss Ellen Cooper-Dean.

Surrounded by large comfortable houses standing in gardens full of stately chestnuts and conifers, there is an air of Edwardian country-house cricket here. Interestingly most of the gardens have a gate in the encircling hedge, and one may imagine bewhiskered, blazered guests emerging to engage in the sort of game so well described by Leveson-Gower. Not only that but it is not difficult to include the children, for it is still possible to pick blackberries behind the beer tent.

The pavilion has all the solidity and opulence of the nineteenth century, and it was from its balcony the home team in 1961, having beaten Derbyshire, acknowledged the crowd's congratulations on winning the County Championship for the first time. A some-

From the scoreboard end of the ground at Dean Park, Bournemouth, the massive pavilion with its humbler professionals' pavilion can be seen to advantage against the trees of this prosperous suburb. [following pages]

what different situation obtained here eight years later when because of prolonged and heavy rain the Hampshire team, the Press, even the scorer left the ground. Then on the third day at 5.30 p.m. the umpires decided play was possible! Only one team, Glamorgan, and one ball were available, so the visitors were awarded the match. However on appeal the M.C.C. later reviewed the decision.

The scorebox and press box are housed in what was the professionals' pavilion, a beautifully made wooden building, the ancestor of all Nissen huts. But it is not the only fascinating reminder of the past, for just to the side of the pavilion is a venerable telephone kiosk, like some majestic sentry box, while the pavilion lavatories, (dare one mention such facilities) are almost collectors' items! But to the wicket: as might be expected it is very slow, for the soil is sandy and dry. Not surprisingly W. G. Grace who appeared here, is not remembered for a high score; that must go to R. H. Moore for his 316 against Warwickshire in 1937, or even to A. Bowell and W. H. Livsey for their tenth wicket stand of 192 in the 1921 Worcestershire match.

A corner of the pavilion with its very domestic bay windows, and the interesting telephone kiosk.

PORTSMOUTH

YOU KNOW it is going to be a ground that is different from all the others, for what other entrance could boast an archway dated 1687? This is admittedly not its original location: King James Gate was once across Broad Street, down at the end of the High Street, then it was moved to the R.N. Barracks, till in 1951 it found its final resting place here, though by this time it had lost the Royal Arms and much of the superstructure.

It is a spartan ground, busy all the year with rugby and hockey as well as cricket. For this is the United Services ground, run by the Royal Navy. Everything is well-organised and without much concession to mere attractiveness. Perhaps the tennis courts' rose-garden brings a little, yet in a way it is out of place in this setting. Why even when there is a county match like-as-not the scorers will be sitting in the open at a table; the Press must be content with a caravan; and as for the spectators, well there is not much except the old concrete terracing.

Of course, when the Mayor attends there will be a tent, and the Hampshire Club will also pitch one next door; but do not expect a festival scene for this is no place for such frivolities.

However what it lacks in comforts it makes up in plenty to see. The pavilion is quite respectable with its hipped roof and stilted balconies. Behind it stand the squash courts and the groundsman's house. Much of this group dates from the time the ground was laid out.

This was in the 1870s when the former defensive works that occupied the land were cleared. Convict labour was used to level and drain the surface as well as to build the pavilion's lower part—the upper floor having to wait until 1905.

There seems to have been an atmosphere in those early years somewhat different from that of today. For one thing only officers were allowed to use the ground. Service bands played on match days; the pavilion was ivy-clad; and, nicest touch of all, the scoreboard was operated by two soldiers on the commands of a sergeant.

To the east of the pavilion and Press caravan are the rugby clubhouse and stand, the latter flanked by no less than a dozen or so flag masts. It must be deemed an unfortunate day for the United Services ground when the Portsmouth Polytechnic was given the planning permission to build those two great slabs of grey and white concrete. For now it is only just possible to see the bright-green domed tower of the law courts and its companion classical-pedimented Guildhall tower. Maybe neither of those has great age to recommend it,

The United Services Ground at Portsmouth, looking towards the city centre [following pages]

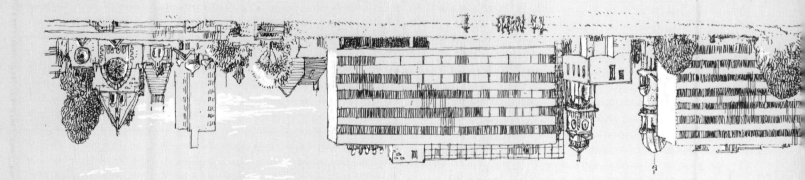

but as features on the east side of the ground their contribution has been sadly diminished.

So you have to content yourself with the rose-windowed façade of the disused church which stands to the south; or, if your eyesight is keen, the silver domes of the distant Palace Cinema, built it is said in the 1920s by an architect fresh from visiting the Khyber Pass. Fortunately steps are being taken to preserve this oriental extravagance, for Portsmouth can do with such eccentricities.

On the south side beyond the tennis courts can be seen the old Nuffield Club known to thousands of servicemen, and now part of the Polytechnic; then west of it the squash courts, before the conspicuous Polytechnic library. Another building to note is that to the south-west: the gymnasium of what was H.M.S. *Nelson*. In 1979 it was in the process of being repaired, and indeed might well take its place as part of the Royal Navy's new sports complex that is to occupy the large area on the other side of Burnaby Road opposite the Memorial Gate. Incidentally it is worth looking at the railings which enclose the area, for they carry the pineapple motif so fashionable after Rose, the royal gardener, had presented Charles II with the first pineapple grown in England.

For many a player the most notable feature of the United Services ground is not the building or the setting, not the regular punctuation of the trains that have a moment or two of free cricket as they rumble along the embankment on their way to Portsmouth Harbour Station, not the movable scoreboard—but the Roller. Every county ground has its heavy roller; no other ground has one like this. It is the grandfather of all rollers. Today it has a V-8 cylinder engine developing, as they say, 350 horse-power, and it is at least the third this 5½-ton monster has had. In the 1920s it was true horse power, for the animal had to wear special leather shoes to protect the pitch.

Stranger sights than that will have been seen on this ground. In 1883 the Iroquois Indians took part in a game of lacrosse with a Canadian team; and in 1904 here was held a Lady Motorists' Race, which included among its requirements that of changing a sparking-plug.

But back to the cricket: the saying 'full of runs' must surely apply here, yet it is reported that there have been fewer drawn games than elsewhere. The first county game, against Sussex, was in 1887, though the first match of first-class status had to wait till 1895 when Hampshire met Leicestershire. A memorable individual score on this ground is P. Holmes' 302 not out, for Yorkshire in 1920; but it is the number of fine partner-

The renowned heavy roller at Portsmouth.

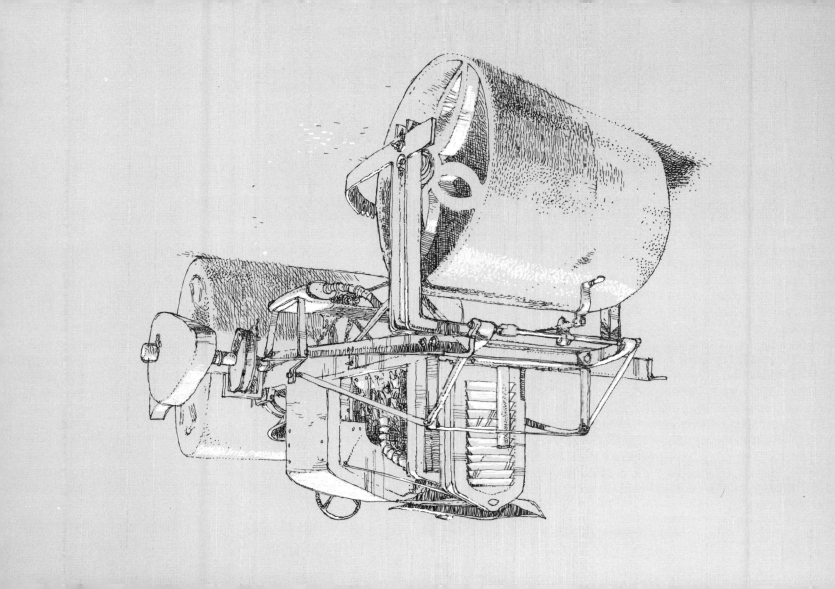

ships that deserves noting. That of R. E. Marshall and J. R. Gray in 1960 against Middlesex when they put on 249 for the first wicket; the 344 for the third wicket by C. P. Mead and G. Brown in the 1927 Yorkshire match; and the 235 for the fifth wicket by G. Hill and D. F. Walker against Sussex ten years later will represent Hampshire's record; while in 1948 the Derbyshire pair G. H. Pope and A. E. G. Rhodes took 241 off the home bowlers in an unbroken stand for the seventh wicket.

Yet it must be the 316 scored in one day by Warwickshire's R. Moore that is most interesting, for on that very same 28th July, at Hove, E. Paynter made 322 for Lancashire; and no other day has seen two batsmen perform such a feat.

Portsmouth's impressive entrance: the gateway of 1687 which was moved here in 1951.

Kent

St. Lawrence Ground, Old Dover Road, Canterbury
CT1 3NZ

IT WAS in 1859 that the county club first was formed, though reorganisation in 1870 was such that the centenary celebrations were based on the second date. From the first it considered itself to be one of the leading counties, and it should be added that the first fully recorded match of 1744 showed that Kent could beat All-England.

It is strange to note that of the Championship matches of 1880, only one of the five home fixtures was at Canterbury, the others being shared equally between Mote Park, Maidstone, and Tunbridge Wells, though the latter would not have been at the Nevill ground. By

1930 the range of grounds had increased. Canterbury had three matches, including the Australian visit; the Weeks at Tunbridge Wells, Tonbridge's Angel ground, Folkestone, Maidstone, and Dover's Crabble ground were now established with two matches each, Blackheath and Gravesend having one match in July and August respectively. Folkestone also was the venue of an England XI v Australia match in the September. Fifty years later the pattern is similar, with Weeks at Canterbury, Maidstone, Tunbridge Wells and Folkestone, while Dartford now has one match instead of those others in the north of the county.

Club colours are red and white. The white horse of the ancient Kingdom of Kent, its proud motto 'Invicta', has been adopted as the emblem.

CANTERBURY

IT WOULD go without saying that, for the Man of Kent or Kentish Man, the St Lawrence ground must occupy the place that Stratford does for the theatre-goer. Here more than anywhere else in Kent, and remember at one time or another there have been some half-dozen or more grounds in regular use, the hopes, the near-adulation, the rejoicing as well as the despair, the acrimony and the devotion have been focused.

There could hardly be a more worthy place. It is of course with the Canterbury Cricket Week that the ground really shows itself to perfection. Even in dull weather, under a rain-filled sky, or buffeted by high wind, the scene is memorable; in August sunshine it is idyllic. And on Ladies Day, the Thursday, there can be no cricket ground to compare with it. The generous sweep of marquees, the bright dresses, the band, the tree and the flags—in the combination of these, and more, rests the magic.

First then the marquees, for it is they which are such an important feature. There is the Mayor of Canterbury's, with its proud flag bearing the arms with motto '*Ave Mater Angliae*', and the Chamber of Trades to represent the city; the County Club has a tent for its president and committee; the Association of Kent Cricket Clubs will be recognised by its flag of green and red stripes; and then there is the Band of Brothers tent.

That of the Old Stagers is a reminder of the fact that Canterbury Week is older even than the St Lawrence ground, for this group of actors traces its origin back to 1842, when the cricket was on the Beverley Club's ground, and they decided to put on a theatrical production. It was an important year also for at the end of that successful Week it was decided to form a Kent Cricket Club. It is interesting to note that one of the Old Stagers some three years later suggested forming a nomadic club for amateur cricketers, and thus I Zingari was born. Its contribution to the game, like that of the Band of Brothers, has been considerable; for example the insistence on not employing professional bowlers did much to counteract the predominance of the batsmen in first-class cricket, where amateurs scored runs and professionals took wickets.

Then of course there is the tent for the Association of Men of Kent and Kentish Men—to clear up the matter let it be stated that Men of Kent are those born east of the River Medway. The Buffs' tent recalls the long connexion that famous regiment had with the county; as every military historian knows, The Royal East Kent's could number Sir Philip Sidney amongst the earliest officers, and as most of Canterbury knew in 1955 the King of Denmark was their Colonel-in-Chief, for in May of that year on this ground he presented new Colours to the 1st Battalion.

There are other tents to identify rather more readily: that of Whitbreads, Gulf Oil, Rotary, and the Conservative Club. No longer do private individuals entertain their guests, though the last tent, Mrs Wheler's of

The pavilion and the Frank Woolley stand from the Annexe, at Canterbury.

Otterden, survived till after World War II.

Important though the tents are, with their flags, the banks of flowers, even carpeted floors, their long tables gleaming with cutlery, china and crisp cloth, the multi-coloured canvas chairs, and that indefinable yet distinctive cricket ground murmur, a low yet completely audible buzz of conversation combining with the clink of glasses, there is much else to see.

Perhaps the most famous feature of all is the tree—some call it a lime—that stands within the playing area. In this it is unique among the county grounds, and fortunate is the fielder who has the advantage of its shade. There was a time when its condition appeared far from healthy, but now it seems to be flourishing and should provide for many years to come an easier boundary for the batsman who succeeds in sending the ball to its ample trunk. Old men will aver that K. L. Hutchings was once caught off a skied hit that dropped from branch to branch into the waiting hands of the fielder.

If Canterbury is alone in having the tree, what of the tomb? Surely this must be another unique feature of this ground. Admittedly it is not in its original location, but it could be argued that St Lawrence's is as appropriate as

From the shaded interiors of the tents the view of the play is never diminished.

St Gregory's for the memorial to Fuller Pilch. Though not born in Kent he made it his home from the age of 31 playing as a member of that team which included legendary men like Alfred Mynn and Felix. In 1847 he was appointed first groundsman at St Lawrence, and for over twenty years he looked after its well-being. He is best remembered as a batsman. In 1922 a bronze portrait of him at the wicket copied from G. F. Watts' famous lithograph, top hatted but without pads, was fixed to the memorial. Today that bronze is to be found in the committee room, but a plaster cast has been on the front of the pavilion for years.

And today that pavilion is called after another person who in a very different way served the club, for Stuart Chiesman gave much of his time and fortune in the lean years after World War II. No longer do the players use a tiny changing-room and eat in the main part crowded

Fuller Pilch's memorial, with that to Colin Blythe, stands amongst the cars and appropriately on the ground he loved at Canterbury.

The full glory of the scene at St Lawrence ground during Canterbury Cricket Week cannot be drawn or described, only experienced. This attempt but indicates some of the features: the tents, flags, the tree. [following pages]

with photographs and paintings; the fine 1970 extension joins the pavilion to the annexe built in 1909, and there is plenty of space for everything. Here you may now see displayed the pads—and snuff box—of Pilch, the shrapnel-riddled wallet of Colin Blythe, the bat that L. E. G. Ames used to score his century of centuries, the bats of F. E. Woolley and M. C. Cowdrey.

This ground does not forget its heroes. On the outside wall of the pavilion carved plaques recount the achievements of the most famous. The concrete stand of 1927 is now the 'Frank Woolley'—maybe it is right that a stand built in the year the Nursery was moved from Tonbridge to Canterbury should commemorate one of Tonbridge's greatest sons. Across the field the old 'iron stand' of 1901 looking very different today with sixteen boxes bookable for the season, bears the scoreboard and the name 'Leslie Ames'. And the memorial to Blythe and his World War comrades still stands by the entrance road.

Yes, Canterbury has changed much since 1896 when the club bought the ground, with its only building a thatched shed. New concrete terracing takes the place of rough planks, bright paintwork gives the solid balustrades and the classical detail a sparkle. Now the press and scorers have glass screens to protect them a little from the south-west winds. Like Chelmsford, the ground acts as a helicopter landing area, for the Kent and Canterbury Hospital whose concrete tower rises behind the line of trees to the west.

But some things do not change. The players still practise on the field before the day's play; the small boys still defend their 'wickets' during the intervals, though doubtless they imagine themselves other than those I have mentioned. And let it never be forgotten that at least one great Kent batsman was 'discovered' because he defended his lemonade bottle better than the others. It is still possible to see the cathedral—and the university now—from the top of the stairs to the annexe; still possible to park a car on the grass embankment and watch the game; still possible to enjoy the cricket and the military band—thus the list could be extended, for this is Canterbury.

And what of the field? It still has that 9-foot slope to the north-east, making the ball race to the boundary, and giving after heavy rain problems for the ground staff. It is a 'sporting' wicket offering opportunity for both batsman and bowler. That is why in 1946 it was chosen as the best place for a Test Trial match. Perhaps also, one might like to suppose, that is why the First Test against the West Indies was held here in 1979—I mean of course the ladies series!

At a ground so full of history you might expect a long list of wonderful matches, great feats of batting or bowling, exciting finishes and indeed the whole spectrum of cricket's drama. Yes, there have been these things though not with the frequency enjoyed by other, lesser, grounds.

In 1862 E. M. Grace, aged 21 years, was reluctantly cabled by his father to travel from Bristol to Canterbury and help out the M.C.C. even though not a member. He arrived during the Week and was bowled first ball in his first innings. In the second he scored 56 runs. It was in the subsequent match against Kent that he showed the meaning of being brother of the Champion for he carried his bat for 192, took five wickets in the first innings and all ten in the second! In 1876 the Champion himself outshone all others in making for the M.C.C. no less than 344.

But enough of visitors' prowess; what of Kent's? Here are some examples for restoring Kentish pride. And who better than Woolley, the Pride of Kent, to start with: in 1923 he scored 270 against Middlesex, out of 445 in the first innings. Dare one reveal that Kent in the event lost the match by seven wickets! Here Ames scored 131 against Middlesex in 1950 to make his hundredth century: his driving and running belied his 45 years, I can vouch for it, as I saw every ball. Here in 1949 D. V. P. Wright celebrated August Bank holiday weekend with yet another of his seven hat-tricks, as Freeman had done twenty-nine years before. Here M. C. Cowdrey scored two centuries against the Australians in 1961, and B. Luckhurst repeated the performance in 1968 against the Rest of the World side.

If ever a ground expressed cricket at its finest, my choice would be Canterbury—but then what else can you expect from a Man of Kent?

TUNBRIDGE WELLS

FOR MOST cricket grounds their attraction and appeal rest in a number of ways, so that it is difficult to isolate one feature as overriding the others. However, such generalisations are made to be refuted, and the Nevill at Tunbridge Wells ably does it. Ask, if you wish, any player what it is that he remembers about this ground and the answer will come quick as a sharp return to the wicket-keeper, "The Rhododendrons". He may of course elaborate a little and mention the colours; if he is afflicted by that cruellest of all complaints for a cricketer he may add "Hay fever". But nobody is likely to cogitate and frown trying to recall the Nevill.

It is a beautiful ground even when the rhododendrons are over, for the grass remains so fresh, and the brilliance of the white paintwork against the luxuriant foliage is given an added intensity by the duck-egg blue of the sightscreens.

When it is Tunbridge Wells Week the tents are to be seen contributing that characteristic Kent grounds sequence. Usually seventeen line the north side of the field, and many of them will be familiar to those who have been to Canterbury. Others are of more local significance: the Blue Mantles Cricket Club, which dates from 1862 and thus is very much older than this ground; the Tunbridge Wells Cricket Club; and rightly the Mayor.

The first county match at Tunbridge Wells was in 1874, but in those days the Common was the venue, that is, Linden Park Club's ground. A pity the Nevill cannot claim the excitement of the following year's match when North met South and W. G. Grace was out first ball. In fact the first three wickets fell in the first four deliveries of the day's play before many spectators had arrived. Tunbridge Wells had its first Week in 1876, and in 1901 the Nevill supplanted the Common.

The stands each side of the pavilion date from about this time, that on the north being known as the Ladies stand, and that on the south as the Sussex stand, for the county boundary once ran through the ground, thus

---

The Sussex stand at the Nevill Ground, Tunbridge Wells gives a fine view of the pavilion and the field, not to forget the rhododendrons.

making it possible for both teams to play at home when it was Kent v Sussex, or, I suppose, Sussex v Kent!

In the pavilion there are photographs of the ground in 1901, and 1908, but the pavilion itself is a different one. Many reasons are cited for pavilions being rebuilt; the Nevill must provide the strangest, for it was the 13th April that saw the old one here burned down by—suffragettes. Maybe it was a blessing, for the new one is an elegant building with its gables and solid timbering, though I fancy the telephone kiosk was there before the fire.

There is a fine view of the wicket from the tiny balcony, across to the bank of rhododendron bushes that conceal the railway line to Hastings, yet give the spire of St Peter's due prominence. To the right there are tennis courts and beyond rises the junior ground which serves as a car park during the Week.

It is a slow-drying wicket, and as you might expect the ball swings in this hollow. Yet the bowlers in the Somerset match of 1911 gave few problems to Woolley, for he scored 104 and 148 not out.

In 1914 James Seymour made 214 against Essex, while in 1934 W. R. Hammond showed his disdain for Kent's bowlers by scoring 290 of Gloucestershire's 563. In 1949 the Sussex innings was 482 to which Kent replied with 237 and 379, B. Edrich contributing 193 not out.

Perhaps the most extraordinary match was in 1963

when, on the Monday morning, Middlesex had to declare 29 runs behind, because traffic congestion had prevented seven of their players from arriving in time to bat. One can but conjecture that if it had not been the Nevill they might well have given up?

MAIDSTONE

IT IS to be found in a park, not a municipal park or a recreation ground but a real park. There used to be deer and many more trees, yet even the disappearance of these has not diminished the sense of being in the grounds of a country house.

The Mote is undeniably a beautiful setting for cricket, or indeed rugby for there are three terraces, created in 1908, with the middle one the cricket field.

Beyond the trees on the far side of the ground from the pavilion a glimpse of the great house is still to be had. Built at the turn of the eighteenth century for Lord Romney, its somewhat forbidding aspect is understandable when you learn that the architect, D. A. Alexander, was also responsible for Maidstone and Dartmoor prisons. However there the similarity ends, as today it serves as one of the Cheshire Homes.

The pavilion has a very Kentish appearance with tiled roof hipped no less than six times, and a central gable bearing the clock. Above it is the scorebox, hardly big enough for even one scorer, and entered along a precipitous catwalk. Inside, the painted boards commemorating the presidents and captains of the Mote Cricket Club date back to 1857; there is a portrait of Lord Cornwallis, captain of the Kent XI for three years; and a plaque over the door tells us that the pavilion was erected in 1910 by "Sir Marcus Samuel Bart, created Lord Bearstead of Maidstone 15 June 1921". The extension at the back had to wait some fifty years.

There is not much else in the way of covered seating. On each side of the pavilion there are members' enclosures, fenced-in as if waiting for the sheep dog, and to the north concrete terracing which used to have the added refinement of a tarpaulin roof.

On the opposite side of the field stands the somewhat primitive scoreboard with another fenced enclosure for players' wives. Of course, being a Kent ground, during the Week there are tents filling half of the perimeter, while on the remainder the terrace of grass affords great facility for viewing.

I have saved till last the most delightful building here. It is a tiny pavilion, richly constructed of wood with the infill spaces displaying beautifully coursed bricks. The verandah has a turned balustrade and even the gables have gothic trefoils to provide a mix of medieval Tudor and classical motifs. This was Lord Bearstead's private ground pavilion, and he bequeathed it to the Band of Brothers, that club formed in 1858. Given the affectionate nickname of the 'Tabernacle' it passed to the Mote Club after World War II, and during the Week serves as K.C.C.C. office. Its interior is as evocative of the past as its outside. There is a fireplace, kitchen, serving-hatch and best of all two marble wash basins that must be original. Even the carpet on the main room's floor is of interest for it came from the council chamber in Maidstone.

Despite new buildings in the park—a swimming pool and sports centre—the scene is still as rural as you could wish for, and fortunately the North Downs retain much of their wooded skyline.

Now to the 'occasions': the wicket has at times been a batsman's, witness the fine partnerships that A. E. Fagg, L. J. Todd and L. E. G. Ames produced in 1947, 273 for second wicket; and in 1949, 251 for first wicket; or Fagg's 136 and 117 not out against Essex in 1948; and the 532 again against Essex in 1950 when Ames, P. Hearn and H. A. Pawson all contributed centuries.

It was here in 1973 that M. C. Cowdrey joined his Kent predecessors Woolley and Ames in scoring a century of centuries. Maybe not many saw that, but thousands, on their television screens, must have seen the BBC helicopter arrive with the John Player League trophy at the nail-biting end of the 1976 season. Incidentally it landed on the wicket instead of the lower terrace!

DARTFORD

THERE are, in all of the cricket counties, small grounds which for one or two matches each season enjoy the passing glory of a first-class visit. Not for them the continual presence and status of capped players, coaches or county secretaries. The rest of the year sees them as club grounds, relishing a game that is different—neither better nor worse—than that which can be seen on the county grounds. They do not have the grand pavilions or concrete terraces; no sponsors' boxes or indoor schools are here. Their moment of glory means the importing of seating, advertisement boards, refreshment tents. Car parks have to be created by roped avenues, tables and 'sentry-boxes' appear for the army

---

Mote Park, Maidstone, with its two pavilions: the small private one of Lord Bearstead, and, beyond, the many gabled structure also his gift; the North Downs rise behind the mature trees of this beautiful place. [following pages]

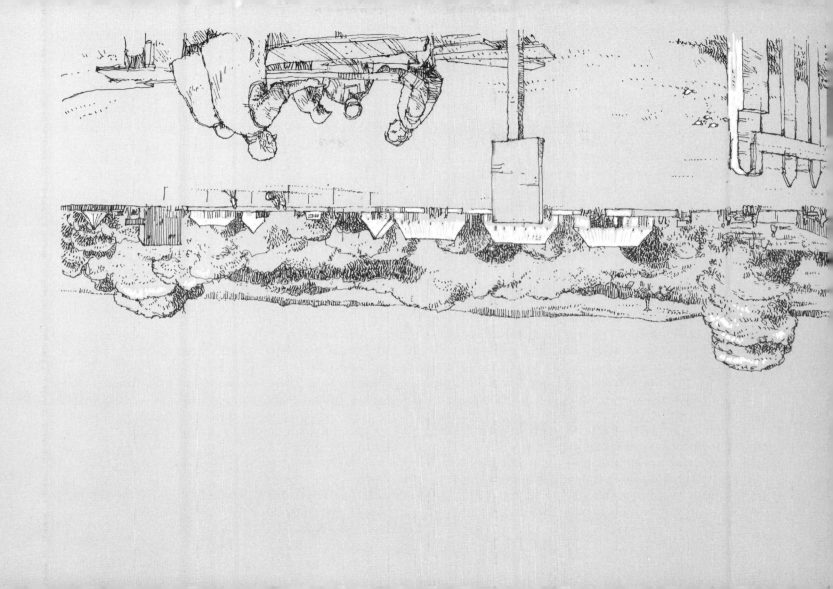

of gatemen and attendants. For a few days these grounds have greatness thrust upon them, and splendid they rise to accept it.

Hesketh Park, Dartford, may represent them. Yet in another way it is the most unrepresentative. For this ground, on the outskirts of London is the rightful successor of Dartford Brent, an area of common, where on 29th June 1709 Kent and Surrey met to play what is reckoned to be the earliest county match on record.

How strange then that it was not until 1956 that county cricket regularly came to Dartford. Perhaps the use of Rectory Field, Blackheath, and the Angel at Tonbridge, not to mention Maidstone, was enough during the preceding years. Anyway when the ground was chosen a new pavilion was built, not at the expense of the old, for that still stands, and indeed becomes the Press box during county matches.

The ground is part of Hesketh Park, which, like Chesterfield's Queen's Park, has ornamental gardens and tennis courts. It was the gift of Everard Hesketh who, being a total abstainer, stipulated that no intoxicating liquor should be sold on the ground. So when the new pavilion was built in 1956 the borough council purchased from the water authority a small piece of land at the end of the ground, thus permitting the pavilion to be only half on Hesketh's gift, so ensuring that the bar in the rear would not break the covenant. Indeed, the public beer-tent also is on the 'Water-Board ground'.

In 1967 the late Bert Lock, M.C.C. Inspector of Pitches, pronounced that Hesketh Park was unsuitable for county matches, but such was the enthusiasm and skill of everybody from the head groundsman down that by 1970 recognition was restored. A result of this attention was the gentle nature of the wicket, which made it a batsman's dream. Hence in 1975 Worcestershire made 468; and C. Lloyd of Lancashire so enjoyed himself with big hits that a lady living nearby felt obliged to dial 999 when her house came under attack.

The first county match in 1956 was against Essex and it is interesting that the first delivery, the first wicket and the first 'six' were all credited to a New Zealander. Even more extraordinary were the events in the 1959 match: Glamorgan having batted well seemed, on the second day likely to have only nine Kent wickets to take, as D. Halfyard had returned from Dartford Hospital on crutches with a leg in plaster. Yet at the end of the Kent innings, out came Halfyard to bat, and soon afterwards he opened the bowling.

Dartford Cricket Club use this ground, as indeed do hockey teams, and it is worthwhile to remind ourselves

Looking across to the old pavilion at Hesketh Park, Dartford, with the newer if less attractive pavilion on the right.

of the debt the Counties owe to such clubs for players. Here the club may claim to have provided a county vice-captain, wicket-keeper and batsman, an England wicket-keeper and an England fast bowler.

It will be a sad day for cricket when such grounds as Hesketh Park are no longer considered able to host both the club and county.

FOLKESTONE

ONE OF the attractions of cricket grounds can be the view beyond the stands. Sometimes it is their good fortune to have a landscape that is so grand that it compensates for the sparseness of the more immediate scene. The Crabble ground at Dover had dramatic slopes enabling the spectator to enjoy almost a bird's eye view of the field, but since it ceased to be a first-class venue, it must be Folkestone alone that commands a panorama from its pavilion hard to equal.

Spread across the skyline the North Downs rear, with the vast bulk of Caesar's Camp as a centre piece, its

From the pavilion of Folkestone's Cheriton Road ground the broad sweep of the North Downs has Caesar's Camp as a central feature.

slopes engraved with chalk paths like string round a pudding cloth. Trees encircle its base and march towards the spreading tide of new houses that seems to threaten the very ground itself.

Despite its northward aspect, the 1926 pavilion with the two curved stands have a seaside air. Perhaps it is something to do with the red pantiles and rough concrete, or the chinoiserie of the balustrades; maybe it is the bright clear light which even the roar of traffic along the Cheriton Road cannot dull; or the spectators who here have a specially holiday character. Certainly sea-mists are noteworthy only because they are rare.

The first Cricket Festival dates from 1925 when a Gentleman *v* Players match was held in September, and two years later county cricket arrived here. A. P. Freeman took 17 Warwickshire wickets for 92 runs in 1932, and in 1949 it returned to enjoy varied support from this part of Kent. The ground had always been quick drying thanks to the sand under that mere 6 inches of top soil. The football pitch area to the north west gave ample car park space, the scoreboard erected in 1938 was ready to display Kent batsmen's achievements, all it needed was a good crowd to make Folkestone Week a success.

Memorable matches were not long in coming. In 1951, Derbyshire found itself the unwilling recipient of a spell of bowling by F. Ridgway that lost them four wickets in as many deliveries. I recall a nice touch by Dawkes the wicket-keeper who firmly closed the pavilion gate as he went out, to stop the succession of batsmen returning. D. Halfyard too had his success, in 1957 he achieved the hat-trick against Worcestershire. Some six seasons later Derbyshire again appeared here, to see D. Nicholls score 211 off them, and in 1966 in the Gloucestershire match A. Ealham held no less than five catches in the deep field off Underwood's bowling.

But surely Folkestone will be remembered for those two matches in 1970. At the beginning of July that season Kent was bottom of the County Championship table. In the match against Nottinghamshire Kent won by three wickets with eight balls left; in the second game against Leicestershire, the home side made 421 for 7, and Underwood took 6 Leicestershire wickets for 53, giving a win for Kent by an innings and 40 runs. From then on the county never looked back, and in its centenary year the Championship came home after fifty-seven years. Folkestone was not the most historic of Kent grounds but it justified its place in the Cricket Festival Weeks on that year's events alone.

Lancashire

Old Trafford, Manchester M16 0PX

THE CLUB began in 1864 and like the other leading sides formally dates its status from the beginning of the Championship in 1873.

In the 1880 season Old Trafford exclusively was used for the six home matches, but by 1930 Liverpool's ground at Aigburth had gained a foothold in the fixture list including incidentally one of the two matches the county played that season against the Australians. Nevertheless, apart from these and one match at Nelson, all the others were at Manchester, where, in the July, the Fourth Test took place also. In 1980 Blackpool and Southport appear with one match each, Liverpool again

has one, while Old Trafford stages nine together with a Test Match.

The Club colours are red, green and blue; the emblem naturally the Lancastrian red rose.

MANCHESTER

THE TRAIN rattles its way from Piccadilly, through Oxford Road and Deansgate Stations, the unwary or first-timers getting out at Old Trafford. For the knowing it is the next stop, Warwick Road, that gives first sight of the famous ground, bleak and windy as the platform may be.

It is the pavilion which identifies the place, though its turreted façade is deprived of some majesty by the imitation classical tower of Stretford Town Hall rising behind. That feature dates from 1931, but since then many more additions to the skyline have come: to the east Portcullis House serves H.M. Customs and Excise—Manchester Docks not being far away, on the

The historic panorama of Old Trafford seen from the west, with Stretford Town Hall behind the pavilion, and the railway station of Warwick Road away to the right of the picture. [following pages]

west the 'modernistic' tower of the DIY and Garden Centre, and on the south four office blocks which recognise the presence of cricket in this grey industrial landscape by their names: Duckworth, Statham, MacLaren and Washbrook.

More indeed may follow, for a hundred-bedroomed hotel with taverns for club members as well as the public is proposed. It will have a scoreboard together with facilities for broadcasting and the Press.

However much the pavilion may be dwarfed by these developments it has stood proudly since 1894, the copper domes, the dark brick and the black stone symbolising that spirit of Lancashire defiance. During the Second World War the ground suffered bombing, but as a result the repairs gave opportunity for improvements and extensions. Today there is a fine committee room with bow window giving a wide view of the play, a president's room, dining-room, library, and Long Room comfortably carpeted and curtained. One interesting touch of northern carefulness is the seating for the players' dressing-room, none of your new plastic and tubular steel here but good old plush and cast iron—for this came from a Manchester cinema.

More of the seats can be found in the scoreboard stand to the west, and how suitable it seems there, for originally it was the dressing-room for club games before it had rooms for the committee and wives.

Doubtless the deep studded-backed seats in the bow-window committee room have greater appeal. Since 1977 ladies have been allowed in the pavilion, so it may not be all that long before the distinction between Members and Lady Subscribers disappears.

There is much here for everybody. Certainly there is plenty of space. The vast expanses of open terraces make the covered stands as islands in a sea of blue. At one time it was intended to have a second tier but this was abandoned; perhaps 24,000 capacity was deemed sufficient, even when it is recalled that in 1926 for the Roses match 78,000 attended—46,000 on the bank holiday—and for five days in 1961 over 120,400 people watched the Test Match here. The legacy of this intention is to be seen in the cavernous walkways underneath the stands, almost like walking round the Colosseum. And not only the stands, but the pavilion, too, has these echoing vaults.

The oldest stand, and strangely the only one to bear a name as well as the designatory letter, is the Hornby. It enjoys an enviable view down the pitch, particularly from its highest seating which rears dramatically over the encircling brick wall of Warwick Road. The adjacent Stand E was built by the ground staff and shows that

Old Trafford has in its pavilion a Long Room worthy of the mementoes it contains.

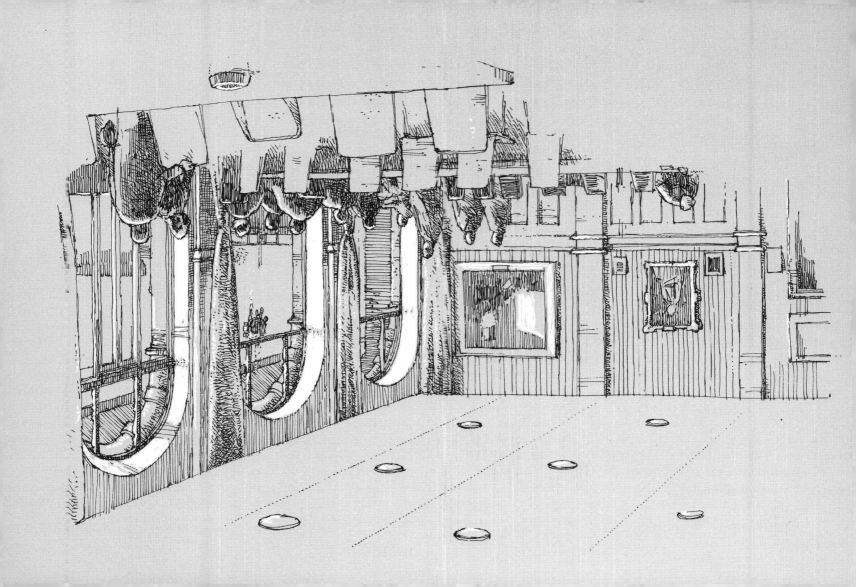

their skill was not confined to providing beautiful turf, for it has survived since 1951.

There has been first-class cricket here since 1865, and Test Matches since 1884. The rich history of this ground includes most of the greatest names in the game. Those Lancashire heroes A. C. Maclaren, A. H. Hornby, and J. T. Tyldesley for example come together in the remarkable game of 1904 against Somerset when they, together with W. R. Currell, scored centuries. It was J. T. Tyldesley who plundered the Kent bowling two years later to make on his own 295. But then with a name like that what else could be expected? Another Tyldesley, E., scored 256 in the Warwickshire match of 1930; while two years earlier he had shared in a second wicket stand of 371 with F. Watson, and this laid the foundations of a daunting 588 for 4 against Surrey. It must however be admitted that this time it was Watson who carried his bat for 300.

Other Tyldesleys have made their mark: R. K., W. K., and J. D. who interestingly scored his three centuries at Old Trafford, as well as performing the hat-trick here, twice. J. B. Statham also, some thirty years later, achieved the hat-trick double, while in 1900 J. Briggs took all 10 wickets of Worcestershire for 55

The Committee Room at Old Trafford has a generous bow window.

runs—interestingly Briggs was to retire having scored 10,000 runs and taken 1,000 wickets for Lancashire; and as if that was not enough he once made a century and did the hat-trick in a Test Match against Australia!

Indeed, in the very first county match, V. E. Walker of Middlesex took 10 for 104, and strangely both sides scored 243 for their first innings. The other county match remembered for its bowler's achievement, though perhaps not by Lancashire supporters, was against Kent in 1931 when A. P. Freeman had an innings reward of 10 for 79, repeating his 10 for 131 at Maidstone two years before.

There can be few lovers of the game who have not heard of 'Laker's Match': that amazing example of spin bowling which gave the England bowler 10 Australian wickets in one innings at a cost of 53 runs, and a match total of 19 for 90. The spectators most fortunate were, on that occasion, those in the scoreboard stand for Laker took all his wickets from the Stretford end.

Twenty years later, in 1976, it was England's turn to suffer, this time at the hands of the West Indies, when out of an innings of 126 the extras exceeded the highest individual score.

Yes, the amiable-to-slow Old Trafford wicket has shown its capability of confounding the experts. In 1952, India could achieve but 58 and 82, in one day too. In 1958 Lancashire was shot-out for 27 by Surrey; in

1890 Sussex gathered but 24. Yet R. B. Simpson scored 311 for Australia in 1964, out of 656 for 8; in 1947 C. Washbrook made 251 in the county match with Surrey, and ten years earlier E. Paynter, that little left-hander, took 266 off the Essex bowlers.

It has not been only the wicket at Old Trafford that has held surprises. Manchester's weather, maybe unfairly, is much maligned. In 1934, however, it had the last laugh, when the Test Match was played in 'almost unbearable heat' as Wisden puts it: in the second innings G. O. Allen's opening over produced three wides and four no-balls making it perhaps the longest on record.

What a contrast then in 1971 when the Gillette semi-final match against Gloucestershire went on till nine o'clock, when, it is asserted, the lights on Warwick Road Station blinded the players!

Old Trafford has a place in the history of cricket and in the loyalties of all Lancastrians: witness when the ground was sold by the Trafford Estates in 1898 it was paid for within two years, and the sum involved was a good few thousand pounds.

Visit the pavilion Long Room during even the most minor of matches and you will hear such perceptive comment and friendly assessment of the play that even Neville Cardus, one of the great writers on cricket, would not be ashamed to own.

The county club has played at Aigburth, Liverpool, since the First World War, at Blackpool since the thirties, and at Southport since 1960, but it is Old Trafford that typifies the spirit of Lancashire cricket. Long may it continue.

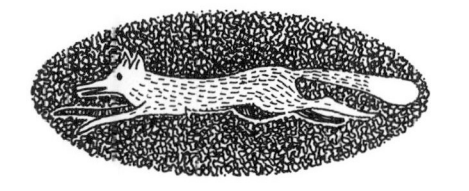

Leicestershire

County Ground, Grace Road, Leicester LE2 8AD

IT SAYS much for a club that, after one year in being, was able to offer home fixtures including a match against the Australian Tourists. And moreover a club that was not deemed first-class until another fifteen seasons.

So, in 1880 there were three matches at Leicester. Fifty years later thirteen were played at Leicester's Aylestone Road ground, one being the Australians match; with both Hinckley and Ashby-de-la-Zouch having one. In 1980 it is Leicester entirely, at the Grace Road ground: twelve, including the West Indies visit.

Colours are scarlet and dark green; the emblem a running fox also on a dark green background. There is little need to explain the significance of colours or emblem for a county typified by its hunting traditions.

LEICESTER

THERE is something fresh even youthful about Leicestershire's ground at Grace Road. Perhaps it has something to do with the light: no overwhelming blocks of offices here, just a skyline of terraced houses, and a row of poplar trees whose gently-waving foliage draws attention to the openness and feeling of space. Perhaps it has something to do with the colours: the tip-up seats on the terracing around the greater part of the ground bring green, red, brown as well as rich black; the bright green roofs of the new stands each side of the scoreboard on the Milligan Road side; the rose beds in front of the pavilion. Certainly the sparkle and freshness may be due to the crisp white fencing that circles the field, provided in 1967 through the bequest of a widow in memory of her husband.

There is a feeling of space too, at Grace Road. At the south or Hawkesbury Road end the grassy bank has behind it trees, looking rather lonely till the new lime trees grow. Here too the car park and nets add their expanse, with only the groundsman's store to take up room.

Everything here seems to be new: stands, seats, even the grass has a scrubbed look about it. But of course it is the pavilion and what is called the Pavilion Suite that is the pride of Grace Road.

The old pavilion had been here since 1889, so in 1966 when the ground at last became the property of the county club a new building arose. Then two years later a connecting Long Room was made between the pavilion and the dining-room. Finally in 1979 the Pavilion Suite completed the complex improvements, with the result that now there are rooms of great variety and indeed interest, for it is an intriguing exercise trying to analyse the development.

The Members' bar is on the ground floor of the 1966 pavilion. It has photographs, club caps and ties to give it a pleasant character, and inevitably the Leicestershire fox is in evidence. On the first floor are the dressing-rooms with the committee balcony; then the second floor has the radio commentary box, and further seating. The exterior is embellished with hanging flower containers and over the main door the most individual of the foxes, this being Joey who had the misfort-

The 'Meet' at Leicester, Grace Road.

une to be despatched during a committee meeting in 1899 by the Billesdon (later the Fernie) Hunt. Still at least he has achieved some posthumous glory, since he can look down on even the most exalted players and members.

In the Long Room and Members' hall, which serves as an indoor school as well as a dining-room, there are many fine displays of memorabilia: bats, balls, blazers, boots once worn by the county's great if under-rewarded bowler G. Geary, plates and paintings, with—wait for it—the omnipresent fox. Because this is a multi-purpose hall there is an uneasy mix of display cases and clinical white walls. Here also are to be found team photos, and those most evocative of all mementoes, cigarette cards. The Press box is above, and then come the sponsors' boxes.

Lastly, almost hanging in space is the Butler stand. You need a head for heights, but it will be worth it for the superb view down the field. And indeed turn and look north too, for then you will have many landmarks of Leicester to identify: the university, the power station, the cathedral's spire, gas holders and cooling towers; while to the south-west the spire of St Peter's, Aylestone. Look up and you will see yet another fox, acting as a weather vane, the survivor from the clock cupola of the Members' dining-room.

If you look once again closely at the field it may be possible still to see traces of the four football pitches, for this ground was used by nearby schools at one time. The effect of this on the surface of the outfield needs no comment.

In fact, Leicestershire has had a rough time with its 'home' in more ways than one. For it is a complicated story. The club began playing county cricket here in 1895. Six years later it moved to the Aylestone Road ground to be nearer the city. But it then found it had a neighbour in the shape of an electricity power station, and the frequent coatings of fine ash were not attractive either, to players or spectators. In 1946 therefore the club returned to Grace Road and for ten years shared its facilities with the education authority's users. Then, back to Aylestone Road for county matches and to the pavilion of 1939. Now there were cooling towers as well. Small wonder then that in 1962 back came the club to Grace Road. And this time it was for good. To demonstrate this the old enclosure stand at Aylestone Road was dismantled, re-erected on the tennis courts side of the ground, given a second storey together with its barn-like roof, and called—yes—the Meet!

It would not be surprising if even close followers found it sometimes confusing, when recalling past triumphs, to decide on which ground they were. There must be a temptation to assert that here Kent was bowled out for 25, that S. Coe made 252 not out, that

W. Watson and A. Wharton put on 287 for the second wicket, but alas that was at Aylestone Road. However at least this ground was spared G. Hirst's 341 for Yorkshire in 1905.

In 1966 the club bought the ground, and, as we have seen, set about its development. The new gates in the north-west corner were erected in 1969, to give a much more dignified entrance, though pedestrians can still use a narrow path running at the side of the 'Cricketers'—an inn which in 1974 replaced the Cricket Ground Hotel.

May there be many feats here to match those of Aylestone Road. Some have already passed into the record books: 1971, Glamorgan bowled out for 24 seems as good an example as any.

But new and exciting as Grace Road looks today it has not forgotten its past and the programme of improvements will not obliterate the evidence of the days of Geary. Why, they still use deck chairs!

The new pavilion complex at Grace Road, Leicester, seen from the steps to the 'Meet'.

Middlesex

Lord's Cricket Ground, St John's Wood Road, London NW8 8QN

FOUNDED in 1863, the club has never had a ground it can call its own. Nevertheless this has not prevented it from enjoying first-class status, and from 1877 the added good fortune to use Lord's.

In 1880, in 1930 and indeed 1980 all home matches have taken place at the veritable headquarters of cricket, the only exception being that Uxbridge had one fixture in 1980, and of course the Test Matches against the Australians have added significance in that 1980 marked the centenary of their appearance in England.

The club colours are dark blue, silver and gold. It is thought that the reason for the club's not adopting the red and gold of the county of Middlesex was that the M.C.C. already used those, and even more confusion between that body and the M.C.C.C. might have arisen. So far as the emblem of the three seaxes is concerned its origin with the Saxons has already been seen in the case of Essex.

Since 1965 the county of Middlesex has ceased to exist, but perhaps it is no more strange for a county side to lack territorial identity than it is for a county to play at home outside its own boundaries—I mean of course Gloucestershire, or Somerset, or Hampshire.

Lord's

WHERE does one start to describe Lord's? First perhaps, to state the obvious: that Middlesex does not own the place, and that M.C.C. stands for Marylebone Cricket Club. Indeed originally the county club had no connexion with Lord's, using a ground at Islington rejoicing in the name New Cattle Market. It was not until 1877 that Middlesex played its first game at 'Headquarters'.

By then the Yorkshireman Thomas Lord had been dead forty-five years; his ground had passed through several owners; the pavilion had been burned and rebuilt, the famous Tavern had been up a decade, and a grandstand had for the same number of years given the spectators a foretaste of the ground that was to develop.

However a Test Match had yet to be played here, and it was not till 1887 that Henderson's Nursery was added to the ground, and gave that term a new meaning in the language of cricket.

Everything at Lord's is large, as might be expected. The Grace Gates set the scale with their massive piers, one bearing the inscription "to the memory of William Gilbert Grace, the great cricketer" and surmounted by carved stumps, bats and balls grouped in the ponderous style associated with the inter-war years classical idiom. Sir Herbert Baker was the designer, and two years later in 1925 his grandstand arose to fill most of the north side.

It is certainly grand, stretching its attenuated façade so wide that the end pavilions seem to have little association with the centre block that incorporates scoreboard and scorebox. When it is full there is an animation about the vast balcony, but at other times the character is one

---

For many a player the Grace Gates at Lord's are the first indication of the ground's particular significance; for Members they are a reminder of tradition.

of a seaside winter gardens. In addition to the seating the building offers boxes, a bar, and printing office. The bar bears the name Father Time, a reference to that feature on the tiled roof which for many symbolises Lord's. This weather-vane, a surprise gift we are told by the architect, has been there since the stand was built, though during the Second World War a barrage balloon cable managed temporarily to unseat the old gentleman.

Of the other stands, whether covered or open top, description can be brief. They have that vastness of seating and anonymity of character that makes it difficult to assign to them a date and harder to find an individuality. Their interest perhaps lies in other aspects.

The Warner stand for example is quite recent by Lord's standards having been erected in 1958. As well as its 3,000 seats, the Press and television commentator's boxes have their place here in the north-west corner of the ground. It is named after one of the happiest of cricketers: a captain of Middlesex who in 1920 led the county to the Championship by a thrilling run of nine successive victories; a man who as captain of England nine years before had had to suffer illness after only one match in Australia; a man who wrote many books on the game,

and who during the Second World War held the position of acting secretary here. It is fitting that he should have formally opened this stand at the place where his first boundary was scored—in 1889.

On the opposite corner is the Mound stand where before 1898 the tennis court could be found. It is the oldest stand on the ground and until 1968 had the famous Tavern to its left. Now that part of Lord's has seen the greatest of changes: the clock tower gone, new stand, new scoreboard.

However the pavilion remains, virtually unchanged since it was built in the year that 'Plum' Warner scored that boundary for Rugby. There, with its squat sturdy roof-line, abounding in cast-iron, terracotta stone richly carved with classic pilaster, it epitomises solid Edwardian confidence and authority. Little seems to have changed, though in 1964 sliding sightscreens were introduced in an attempt to rectify the inevitable disadvantage of a north-east facing building that is in shadow for much of the play. The question must often have been asked, why was the pitch not made parallel to

Nobody who has heard of Lord's can be unaware of the famous Long Room, that model for all other pavilions.

There can hardly be a more familiar, or more impressive, background to cricket than that of the pavilion at Lord's. Even the newer stands and the tower blocks do not diminish the majesty of that centre-piece. [following pages]

the pavilion? After all there were seventy-five years between Thomas Lord's laying the turf and Thomas Verity's design, so it might well have been possible to have a different location. It goes without saying that the pavilion has the committee room, a writing-room and a Members' bar, that on the first floor are the players' dressing-rooms, and that above them there should be a luncheon room, committee dining-room and a lecture room—for so important a building will assuredly have the best appointed facilities.

But it is the Long Room that excites most admiration. Here if you wait long enough you will be rewarded with a sight of everybody who is anybody in cricket. My own experience must be typical of many: to turn round on one day in the 'fifties and find myself looking at A. P. F. Chapman. It is a room with all the heavy grandeur of pedimented doorways, rich cornices, and substantial tables. The walls bear their due share of paintings and showcases, but since the Memorial Gallery was opened the overcrowding has been relieved.

That opening by the Duke of Edinburgh took place in 1953 when the old rackets court behind the pavilion was redecorated and given the slightly antiseptic atmosphere of an art gallery. But despite the harsh light, clinical floors and the neo-classical railing there are good things to be seen here: pads made out of whalebone; Bradman's boots; Hobbs' blazer; photographs of early fast bowlers standing on one leg with arm in air whilst trying to maintain a ferocious expression during the exposure; caps, bats, stamps, china, blazers, paintings of grounds and players including the full-length portrait of F. S. Trueman by Ruskin Spear, one of the minority of modern works.

Everybody visiting this gallery looks for the unfortunate sparrow forever fixed to the ball which despatched it on 3rd July 1936, though at least it has gained a kind of immortality. Ten years earlier, its predecessor, 'John Willy', was an unintentional participant in J. Hobbs' 316, but for him no taxidermist's attention. And of course no visitor leaves without looking at the surprisingly minute urn containing the Ashes.

The Memorial Gallery is not the only collection of cricket memorabilia, for next to it is the library where the bibliographic counterpart is housed. Together these must constitute the richest assembly of material anywhere, and it is reassuring to learn that it is supervised by enthusiastic as well as capable hands. The group of buildings behind the pavilion includes the tennis court, (real, or royal, tennis of course here), while on each side of it two gardens have been laid out. That on the south is known as the Harris Memorial Garden and was opened

---

The Memorial Gallery at Lord's has W. G. Grace to preside.

Two well-known exploits in the Memorial Gallery: the 'Ashes', and the unfortunate sparrow with its lethal ball.

in 1934 in recognition of Lord Harris, a man of forceful character who captained Kent, and who played at Lord's for sixty-one years. His career spanned the age of Kent cricket from E. Willsher to F. Woolley, he made 33 against the West Indians at the age of fifty-five, and at sixty he scored 36 against the All-Indian team. Little wonder he was President of the M.C.C. The garden itself, like him, is somewhat formal, though on occasion it has a luncheon marquee to give a more festive air. Seats around it are memorials to other cricketers. The other garden, on the north side, commemorates the Coronation of Elizabeth II, and is a favourite place for informal meals.

The remaining building at this end of the ground is the New Tavern by the Grace Gates. It is 'New' because it replaced in 1967 the former Tavern so popular with generations of spectators. Very different in its style and materials from that of E. Paraire, the design of D. Hodges may yet become as familiar if not as companionable.

At the Nursery end of the ground, change has not been quite so evident. The clock tower still peeps over the north-corner stand, giving that welcome accent of London brick, and the practice ground beyond which was laid out in 1887 still has some of those quaintly named arbours. In the past they were linked in a delightful series of arches, and featured in many an action photograph.

Since 1977 an indoor school has occupied the southern corner of the car park, itself formed from part of the practice ground and which, as already stated, was once the nursery of Guy and Henderson. Perhaps the most surprising thing is that Lord's had to wait so long for one. Anyway it has made up for the delay by proving to be well-equipped in all respects: seven nets, viewing gallery, bar, even a shop.

Nearby there is another shop, in what was the East Lodge. This is for the general public to buy its souvenirs and favours, as well as more substantial products of the diverse world of cricket publishing.

How fortunate it is that there are still trees to act as a backcloth to the Nursery, and how grateful everyone must be that the trains from Marylebone rumble through a tunnel beneath Wellington Road. It is still possible to hear the evensong bell of St John's Wood chapel, and feel that Lord's has not changed all that much since 1814.

To attempt a comprehensive account of events which have taken place here must be foolish if not impossible. Where does one start and what does one leave out? There was the balloon ascent in 1837 by M. Garnisin, the visit of the Iowa Red Indians in 1844, and the canary shows till 1898; the conversion in the First World War of the pavilion to become a factory making haynets for cavalry horses, the occupation by the R.A.F. in the Second World War, the lacrosse and the hockey—if such occasions are difficult to limit what of the cricket?

Let us start with A. E. Trott who played for England and Australia, as well as Middlesex. He hit a ball clean over the pavilion, in 1899, and in his benefit match against Somerset here he took four wickets in four balls and then the hat trick in one innings. Add to that a batting average of 103 in a Test Series, and it might seem that anything else would be an anticlimax.

Nevertheless—1901, G. L. Jessop made a century in fifty-seven minutes, and 200 in 135 minutes; 1921 F. G. Mann 50 in fourteen minutes; 1924, England 503 for 2 in one day against South Africa; 1930, Australia 729 for 6, of which D. G. Bradman contributed 254. In 1934 the third day of the Test Match proved significant, for more than one reason. It was not just that 14 wickets fell for 80 runs, or that H. Verity had a return of 8 for 43, but that six wickets fell in the last hour. Howard Marshall, the BBC commentator, was so hard-pressed by this that for the next Test he was allowed a scorer-assistant, Arthur Wrigley. Thus the practice was established which has continued ever since. There have been other instances of fine bowling, for example, R. A. L. Massie in his first Test appearance for Australia took 16 for 137; there have been low scores, 42 by India in 1974, 19 by M. C. C. back in 1878, 58 by South Africa in 1912, when the highest score was 'extras'; there have been short matches, like that in 1899 between Middlesex and Somerset which lasted but three hours; there have been freak conditions, like the 1968 Test that was accompanied by a hailstorm. In short, most things have happened at Lords.

Let that perceptive cricketing parson of last century, James Pycroft, have the last words: "Yes, that ring at Lord's shows me every gradation in the scale of life—the once active now stiff and heavy, the youthful grey, the leaders of great elevens passing unrecognised and alone. Every old cricketer knows by sight, and is himself known to hundreds from frequenting Lord's—people who seem to him as distinct and as peculiar to those haunts as if he returned periodically to another land."

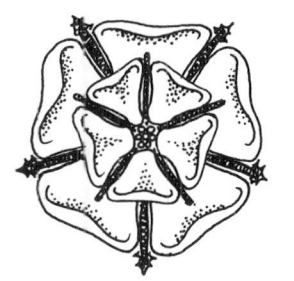

Northamptonshire

County Ground, Wantage Road, Northampton NN1 4TJ

IT IS strange that a club which might claim to be the oldest of all the county ones should have had to wait until the opening decade of this century for first-class status. Northamptonshire was formed in 1820, and although reorganised in 1878 this was no uncommon procedure. In 1890 the County Cricket Council deemed it to be in the third-class category. But, like Glamorgan, it gained its promotion to the County Championship through tenacity and enthusiasm.

Thus, there is no 1880 fixture list to draw on. However in 1930 its Home matches were as numerous as any of its first-class elders, with eleven at Northampton, two each at Peterborough and Kettering. Fifty years later Wellingborough and Milton Keynes have ousted all but Northampton, and indeed it is to the Buckinghamshire town that the West Indies are visitors.

Maroon is the club colour, while its emblem is yet another rose, a flower that occurs more than once on the county arms.

NORTHAMPTON

IT IS doubtful if even the most partisan supporter of Northamptonshire would assert that the county ground at Wantage Road was beautiful. True it is within sight of Abington Park, but the landscape offers little more than the tantalising tops of its trees, and in another direction only the spire of St Matthew's Church—a church worth visiting incidentally for its works by Henry Moore and Graham Sutherland. Otherwise it is a setting of dull brick terraces of houses, a workaday ground with a no-nonsense air about it.

Northampton may not have a beautiful ground, but, as this drawing shows, there is a sturdy character about it. [following pages]

Like many others, it shares the field with other sports, here it is the town's football club. Indeed the north end is known as the Football Ground end, and there will be found the stand together with floodlight pylons.

On the east side is the bowling-green; a feature of some importance for the players has been its pavilion, for when the County Hotel at the north-west corner of the ground ceased to serve as the lunch place it took over the duty.

Between the bowling-green and the old pavilion the scoreboard presents a sideways face to the members. This is an inevitable consequence of the shared ground, as indeed is the field itself where the football pitch overlaps the outfield. Perhaps it is not always appreciated by spectators that a misfield may be the ground's and not the player's fault.

A large pavilion would be out of place here, and the scale of Northampton's seems right, with its little cupola. But since 1979 it has had a successor: a long somewhat featureless building dwarfed by the stand that lies between the two pavilions.

One charming survival is the scorebox, which is used also by the Press, and functions as a cricket shop. With its tiny columns and half-timbered top it looks like a

The view from the old pavilion at Northampton.

cross between a doll's house and a signal box.

Before the indoor school stand and the new pavilion were there, the ground was vulnerable to the south-west winds. But curing one source of discomfort sometimes creates another: the wicket here used to be quick drying, now it is the opposite though favouring the batsman. Perhaps C. Milburn developed his predilection for mighty hits through this, or maybe he was inspired by W. Hammond's example of a six clean over the old pavilion. Similarly it is not unexpected that the record which comes to us from the earlier years is of a bowler taking all ten wickets in an innings: unfortunately for Northants it was C. Blythe of Kent in 1907, in fact his match haul was 17 for 48.

However, when F. R. Brown took over the captaincy of Northants in 1949 there was a transformation, and the side became one of the most exciting and dangerous in post-war cricket. On this ground in 1953 T. L. Livingstone and D. Barrick scored 299 for the second wicket against Sussex; in 1976 R. T. Virgin, the former Somerset player, and P. Willey put on 370 for the fourth wicket against that county; and the fifth wicket record was 347 by D. Brookes and D. Barrick in 1952 in the Essex match. Incidentally, Brookes held the county's record for the most runs in a season, the most in a career and the most centuries.

Yes, there has been good cricket here. It may be an

unbeautiful ground, maybe the entrance resembles more a school playground, maybe maroon is an apt colour for the setting as well as the flag, but Wantage Road will continue to attract the supporters of Northants, and future seasons may well see trees return to the forecourt as well as the cars.

And one event, or conjunction of the unlikeliest, must be that, when P. G. H. Fender in 1920 made a century for Surrey in thirty-five minutes, only a man who once square-cut a ball for six could have chosen Northampton for such a record.

Nottinghamshire

County Ground, Trent Bridge, West Bridgford, Nottingham NG2 6AG

FORMED in 1841, this is one of the doyens of the county clubs. It has always been first-class, and 'Trent Bridge' has been almost synonymous with 'Notts'. Indeed, in the 1880 season this was the only ground used for home matches, and fifty years later the situation was unchanged. A further half-century on, the only exceptions are one match at Worksop and another in the Lincolnshire town of Cleethorpes. Perhaps this out-county 'home' fixture is an indication of future practice, and a small threat to the territorial principle of the Championship. Nottinghamshire is not an isolated instance for it has been noted in other counties: Glamorgan, and Northampton being two, while Gloucestershire, Somerset and Yorkshire are more the victims of county reorganisation.

The club colours are green and gold; the emblem is nothing less than the full achievement of arms, that is, shield supporters and crest of the city of Nottingham.

NOTTINGHAM

CRICKET grounds come into being in a variety of ways: sometimes they are a result of deliberate choice of site; sometimes they are the result of a lucky coincidence of land becoming available and generous benefactor coming forward. Here at Trent Bridge it was neither, or was it both?

In the 1830s William Clarke married Mary Chapman. He was a bricklayer and keen amateur cricketer; she was landlady of the Trent Bridge Inn. Never was a happier alliance contracted, for William had his own nomadic team and here was the ideal site for a cricket field. The story is well-known.

By 1840 the first county match had been played, Sussex being the opponent. For almost a hundred years the inn was part of the club's ground, and indeed served

as its pavilion. Today its successor, built in 1938, still stands at the corner of Bridgford Road and Radcliffe Road, flags bravely proclaiming the existence of one of England's most famous grounds.

It is a friendly ground, possessing that endearing mix of old and new. Some of the buildings owe their origin to the last century, others could hardly be newer.

In 1951 the pride of Trent Bridge was its scoreboard. Nowhere else in the country were there so comprehensively displayed details of batsmen's scores, bowling performances, fall-of-wicket scores; fielders were indicated by numbers and a light came on over the appropriate one when the ball was fielded. Spectators were kept very busy trying to watch both the play and the board. Indeed, the only information which the scorecard might claim exclusiveness in was the umpires' names. But it proved costly to operate, and its maintenance was demanding—hardly surprising when each number was made up of a pattern of revolving balls presenting either a black or white surface.

So in 1972 the gift of Forman's was replaced by that of Ladbroke, and the result is a corner of the ground that continues to have a distinctly Australian character.

Maybe the towering bulk of Trent Bridge House office block behind has something to do with it.

On the opposite side of the Radcliffe Road end a very different character invests the ground. First there is the stand which has the company boxes. It dates from the turn of the century and its elegant cast-iron brackets above the generous windows are reminiscent of those Mississippi river boats. Here were to be found the scorers and Press, but now these first-floor boxes bear honoured names: Voce, Butler, Hardstaff, Keeton, Carr, Simpson, Whysall. Each deserves a paragraph, if not a page, to do justice to the contribution he has made to Nottinghamshire cricket.

Then round the curve in front of the Trent Bridge Inn swings the Bridgford Road stand. It too has charming roof supports, fit for a Victorian conservatory. Next comes Parr stand so named because here, until it was blown down in 1975, stood the elm remembered for the great hit George Parr made.

When the West Wing is reached, that spacious courtyard so much enjoyed by spectators with their refreshment between the Trent Bridge Inn and the Bridgford

---

From the top of the Radcliffe Road stand at Trent Bridge; a better view of the game would be hard to find anywhere else.

The Long Room at Trent Bridge, Nottingham, allows the customary view of the ground so appreciated on cool days. In warm weather Members prefer the seats in front of the pavilion. [following pages]

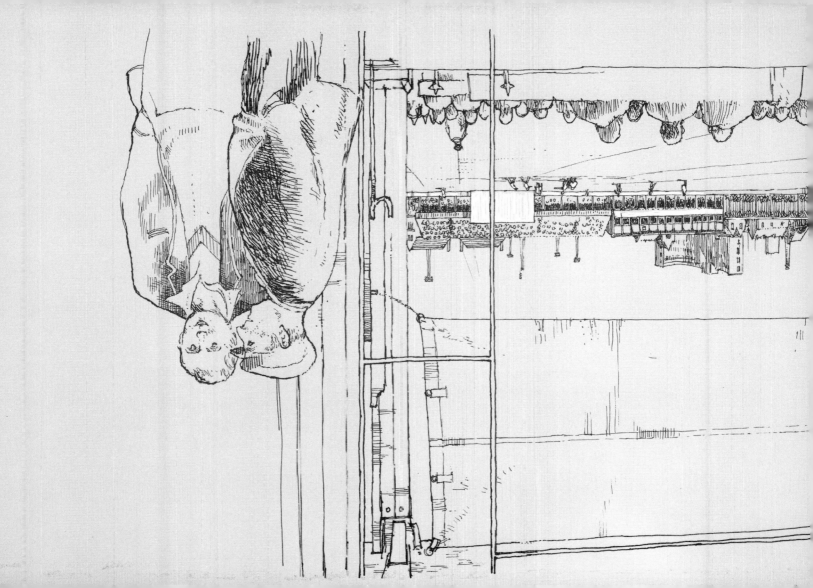

Road stand has dwindled to a narrow passage, before opening out again at the Memorial Gates. Here a rather lonely tree does its best to bring some green relief to the white concrete and Midland brick. On the south side of the gates, which incidentally perpetuate the name of J. A. Dixon, the club captain from 1889–99, the new offices, the indoor school and squash court use up the remaining land before Hound Road.

Directly opposite the gates stands the pavilion, one of the finest in the country. Built in 1886, its generous balustrades, white woodwork, rich red brick and decorative ironwork have all the characteristics of imperial self-confidence. It is a pity that the demands of scorebox and radio and television commentators resulted in the erecting of a permanent extension over the verandah in 1953. But clearly the appearance of the façade had to take second place to the better reporting of the cricket.

Inside, happier alterations have been made. The Long Room, always impressive—the West Bridgford Urban District Council met here as long ago as 1895—looks even grander today with its fine displays of mementoes. There are bats, not least that of V. T. Trumper the Australian who at Old Trafford was the first to score a

The pavilion doorway well-known to players and autograph-seeking small boys.

Test century before lunch. There are mounted engraved balls: F. J. Shacklock's with which he took four wickets in four here against Somerset in 1893; Gunn's 6 for 19 in 1904; Butler's hat-trick in 1937. Most evocative of all are the pads—the last he wore—of Arthur Shrewsbury. All right, there was no love lost between George Parr and Shrewsbury though Gedling churchyard has them both, but who cannot but feel for a man who represented batting at its most diligent; who went to Australia four times, twice as captain; who saved a match by a flawless century after three wickets had rapidly fallen, whom W. G. Grace judged to be inferior only to himself; yet a man who feared the loss of his eyesight so greatly that he took his own life.

In 1979 the room at the back of the pavilion was made into a library, and, since in that year too the ladies' stand was rendered obsolete by removal of any discrimination here, there must be for many a member of either sex an even greater pride in the Trent Bridge pavilion.

But for me the essence of this place is to stand in the west hall and hear the descent of the players from their dressing-rooms, down the stairs, past the ranks of photographs of past presidents and of autograph seekers, finally to depart into the sunlight of the field.

Trent Bridge pavilion is well served with balconies.

Others may prefer the vantage point high up on the pavilion. The city of Nottingham is spread out behind the Radcliffe end: on the right Colwick Park's tree-covered hill; the massive tower of St Mary's Church; the Council House dome; the floodlights of Notts County and Forest football grounds—and it is worth recording that for some eleven seasons Notts County played here, on the Fox Road side of the field—and the squat shape of the castle on its rock.

For many years Trent Bridge had the reputation of being the graveyard of bowlers, a ground where the wicket was a featherbed, and every match ended in a draw. Of course it was only a half-truth. Some said it all started with the appointment of 'Fiddler' Walker as groundsman in 1877, for he generously applied soil from Cotgrave marlpit. Whatever the long-term result was, in the 1950s the table was relaid. Perhaps the gesture of R. T. Simpson had something to do with it, for he bowled under-arm lobs to W. Wooller of Glamorgan, though maybe there was another reason for that—on a previous occasion Wooller had used every player in the Glamorgan side as a bowler, to have that great scoreboard crammed with their analyses!

A ground with so long a history as this is, not surprisingly, rich in records. In 1903 the home side declared at 739 for 7 against their closest rival Leicestershire, J. Gunn contributing 294. Two years earlier Yorkshire had humbled them here by bowling them out for 13, though when the Australians came in 1921 the defeat for Nottinghamshire was by an innings and 517 runs.

Individual scores have frequently passed the double-century here, from J. A. Dixon's 268 not out against Sussex in 1897, A. Shrewsbury's 267 against Middlesex in 1887, and against Sussex in 1890, to R. T. Simpson's 243 in the Worcestershire match of 1950, W. W. Keeton's 261 against Gloucestershire 1934. But it is A. O. Jones who almost reached a triple century in 1903 with his 296. 'Fiddler' Walker has had much to answer for!

Somerset

County Ground, St. James' Street, Taunton TA1 1JT

FORMED in 1875, the club did not achieve first-class status until 1891. Consequently the only home fixture to record of the 1880 season was that at Bath. By 1930 the three principal grounds were established as venues for matches, Taunton as might be expected having eight including the Tourists' visit, Bath having four, and Weston-super-Mare three. Fifty years later Taunton again has eight, with the Tourists, and Bath and Weston, now of course outside the county boundary, still enjoying two matches each.

Black, white and maroon are the club colours. The emblem is the Wessex dragon, standard of the English and shared as the royal badge of Wales. Because it is the forerunner of the wyvern it is sometimes incorrectly thus described. Interestingly, the dragon, which strictly should be red, appears on the club's flag as white with red only on its tongue, and as blue on the players' sweaters. The county arms give the dragon a mace to hold, but presumably a cricketing dragon has to have hands free!

TAUNTON

A GROUND dominated at one end by church towers, at the other by the Quantock Hills, could only be in Somerset. A range of pavilions and stands having a homely, slightly rustic, appearance, and until 1980, a wall of screens supported by the town's old tram-lines, a scoreboard complete with classical pediment over a clock and a delightful air of Victorian cricket—all this presented an image that was so thoroughly that of Taunton, the most south-westerly of first-class grounds. Here was, and is, a town-ground: North Street is a busy shopping centre, and just before the bridge, a narrow St James' Street takes you past the baths and the church to the entrance gates. There are few county grounds so easily reached.

Those entrance gates bear the initials J.C.W., in memory of Jack White. He first played for Somerset in 1909 and it was not until 1937 that he 'hung up his boots'. The intervening years saw this slow left-arm bowler take 100 wickets in a season fourteen times. For him the Quantocks were as familiar as the Taunton ground, but at the age of thirty-seven years he went further afield having been invited to go on the Australian tour of 1928–9. He did not disappoint the Selectors: in the First Test he took 4 for 7 in six overs; in the Third it was 5 for 107, and in the Fourth 13 wickets. There would have been as much jubilation in Stogumber or Combe Florey as in the M.C.C. dressing-room at Adelaide.

It was the Taunton Athletic Co. which secured the place in 1885, and a year later the newly reorganised county club acquired the lease. With the enthusiasm that has always been typical the club set about improving the ground. First the running-track had to be covered, then pavilion and stands erected. So it was not until 1891 that the first county match took place here. From the start, Somerset knew what it would have much of, for Lancashire won.

There is a friendliness about this ground, and indeed a homeliness. On the west side of the Ridley stand Taunton Cricket Club has its own little pavilion; the scoreboard was given by the Somerset Stragglers; and the Supporters Club make their stand at the River end available to the public.

Let us hope that this atmosphere survives the changes that are taking place. A new pavilion will be found on the north-east side, its roof design presenting an interesting contrast with the older range on the south.

The greyhound racing track was till 1979 a feature of the boundary with its lighting, though it was still possible to find evidence of the rail for the 'hare'. Maybe few will regret the passing of this aspect of the ground, but the high screening so much a part of Taunton's scene is going to be missed, for it provided a protection against the north winds and gave spectators in that corner a welcome sun-trap.

But those spectators will not be deprived of the view that distinguishes this ground from all others. The towers of St James's, St Mary's, St George's, even of Holy Trinity; the spires of St John's, perhaps of St Andrew's also, will still contribute to the richness of the scene. On the east the Organ Factory, the printing works, the medieval Priory Barn and the elegant St James's Rectory leads the eye to the characteristic shape

The County Ground at Taunton looking south: behind the old pavilion rise the magnificent towers of St James's and St Mary's Churches; since this drawing was made evidence of the greyhound track has largely gone.

of the Maltings.

Some features have already gone: the stable in the north-west corner where the horse lived that pulled the roller and the mower is but one. But the new will surely give the ground a fresh life. No longer will the players have to change in a room that denies any view of the game; no longer will the Members have to go without their mementoes of the club's past.

For this ground has much to look back on. Only one year after that defeat by Lancashire, H. T. Hewett and L. C. Palairet scored 346 before Yorkshire could take their first wicket. Here in 1946 that other great player from the Quantocks area, H. Gimblett, made 231 against Middlesex. It must have given him as much satisfaction as his century in his very first county match in 1935, made incidentally in sixty-three minutes.

Other counties too have enjoyed Taunton. In 1895 Lancashire again dominated the home side by making 801, of which A. C. MacLaren contributed 424, sharing a second wicket stand of 363 with A. Paul. In 1905 Kent declared at 601 for 8, four batsmen, including the great F. E. Woolley, making centuries. Nearer the present day, P. Spicer of Essex with his first ball received in

Looking north from the Ridley Stand to the gracious skyline of the Quantock Hills.

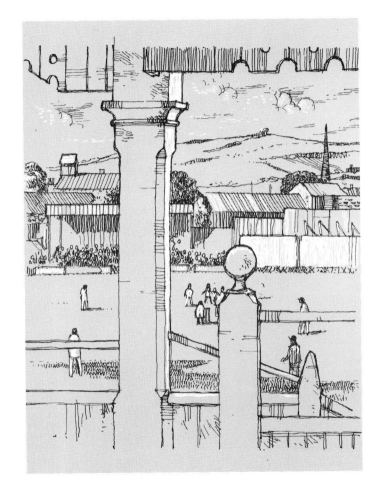

first-class cricket hit a six. Seventeen seasons later, in 1979, M. J. Procter of Gloucestershire scored 93 in forty-six minutes; there were eight sixes in three overs, six of them being consecutive, and G. Sobers' Swansea record might have been equalled had another big hit not been intercepted by a spectacular dive, almost resulting in a remarkable catch.

But surely Taunton will be remembered most for its being the setting for the great occasion in 1925 when, in the first innings of the Surrey match, J. B. Hobbs scored his 126th century to bring him level with the record of W. G. Grace. A glass was brought out to him on the field with the congratulations of players and spectators ringing out. As if that were not enough, in the second innings he scored another century. By strange coincidence it was on this very ground that in 1895 Grace had completed his own century of centuries, and for him the event was celebrated by champagne. It had its effect for he went on to make 288 in 320 minutes. If the new pavilion does not in some way remember those days, then it will indeed be a change for the worse.

Taunton's new pavilion was still just a model at the beginning of the 1980 season but its foundations were firmly laid, an expression of this club's confidence in the future.

BATH

THERE is an appropriateness about a cricket ground in Bath, for the sport and the city grew up in the same century. Although no significantly memorable paintings of cricket have Bath as their setting, it is not difficult to imagine this elegant part of Somerset attracting the society of Beau Nash and Ralph Allen to patronise such men as John Nyren or the Rev. James Pycroft wrote of. It must be remembered, too, that the Prince Regent was himself described as a "noble cricketer and few could bowl him out".

However it was in the latter part of the nineteenth century that County Cricket was established in Bath. The first match was in 1880 against Sussex which the visitors won by a wicket.

The Recreation Ground where the Festival is held has a delightful setting with a fine view of the abbey to the west over the River Avon. Its tower, broader than it is long, unfortunately does not present a convenient clock face for the the umpires to use. So instead of their eyes being directed to the Perpendicular glory of Bishop King, they look in the opposite direction and the church clock of St Mary Bathwick, built somewhat later, at the time of the

Few grounds have so elegant a turnstile as that at Bath.

Battle of Waterloo.

On the Pulteney Road side there are tennis courts which during the Festival accommodate the marquees of local cricket clubs, and south of them a croquet lawn. The opposite side of the ground has the rugby pitch with its spacious stand. But it is too far away from the cricket to be of use, and consequently temporary seating is erected.

At the top or north end the pavilion occupies the terrace and has for company to the west tents for scorers, Press and printer, together with the county secretary's caravan. It is all very homely and small scale.

But, at the bottom, or North Parade, end, things are very different. For since 1972 the sports and leisure centre has occupied the space, and indeed doubtless the minds of many spectators: it was the centre of some controversy when the design came under scrutiny by the Royal Fine Art Commission. Despite the use of such terms as "heavy and monolithic" and "most unfortunate" in siting, the work went ahead. Perhaps one day it will be more in keeping with the locality.

Behind it rises the wooded eminence of Beechen Cliff, its rounded summit contrasting with the spire of St John's R.C. Church in South Parade.

There has been good cricket here, for Bath has been more fortunate than its ground might suggest in attracting the big matches. Because of its greater accessibility than Taunton, it is here that Touring sides have come on occasion. In 1977 for instance the Australians were the visitors, and opportunity was taken to have the captains plant two silver birch trees to the west of the pavilion. Added significance was attached to this as the Australian captain had, years before, played for Somerset.

In 1919 J. C. White took 16 Worcestershire wickets for 83 runs; in 1924 Somerset declared at 675 in the Hampshire match; and 1936 H. L. Hazell hit the Yorkshire bowler H. Verity for twenty-eight in one over. In the Lancashire match of 1958 it was all over in one day, and in 1960 the county record stand for the third wicket was established by G. Atkinson and P. B. Wight when they put on 300 against Glamorgan.

Like many grounds, change is taking place. No better example could be found than in my drawing of 1979 where the line of trees behind the rugby stand is no longer there, having been felled in February 1980. They are to be replaced, it is true, by tulip and willow, but I only hope the delightful turnstile behind the pavilion does not disappear overnight.

Bath Abbey and Beechen Cliff dominate the ground in the most satisfying way. [following pages]

WESTON-SUPER-MARE

FOR THE rest of the year it is simply the unpretentious, workmanlike part of Clarence Park; it is the other side of Walliscote Road that has the flower-beds and the bowling-green. Here ilex and pine bound a very ordinary field. Beyond the grey stone wall suburban houses of similar grey, a church, can be seen, and, at each corner, entrance gates serve to emphasise the sheer ordinariness of it all. There are two municipal shelters, doubtless dating from 1882 when Rebecca Davies presented the land to the town, their cast-iron columns suitably painted in council green. A pavilion, reminiscent of some inter-war bungalow at Peacehaven, stands between the shelters. Head-scarfed ladies walk their dogs, respecting the wired-off square.

But the scene is very different when the county comes to play. Tents appear on the north side for the players, on the south for sponsors and the public. Deck chairs are ranged in front of the pavilion; cars to the north; there are temporary stands, a mobile scoreboard, caravans for the Press, the secretary, the printer; a shed serves as a scorebox; amplifiers take up position on the pavilion balcony; and the advertisement boards encircle the boundary. The ground fills with holiday crowds, though there must be others who seek a free view from over the wall.

The Cricket Festival began in the inauspicious year of 1914, Essex and Yorkshire being the visitors—the third match, against Northamptonshire, being cancelled, doubtless because of the outbreak of war. However, in 1922 three matches returned to Clarence Park, and since then this unassuming ground has been the setting for some fine games. In that year the match against Middlesex gave a splendid foretaste: the visitors' 346 for 6 was followed by 185, while Somerset made 288 and in the second innings claimed extra time, achieving a win, by two wickets, off the last ball, when fifty-one-year-old E. Robson hit a six over the pavilion.

There have been big scores here: 507 against Surrey in 1946, and low too: 36 against the same county in 1955. Individual performances have included M. M. Walford's 264 against Hampshire in 1947; hat-tricks by Hilton and Lomax in 1955 and 1958; E. P. Robinson's 15 Sussex wickets for 78 in 1951; and most extraordinary of all, the Sussex match in 1948, when James Langridge took two Somerset wickets in two deliveries no less than three times, including four wickets in five balls.

Weston-super-Mare may not have a pavilion as impressive as those on other Somerset grounds, but the cricket has not suffered nor support waned.

In the 1930s A. Wellard hit J. C. Clay of Glamorgan
onto the roof of St Paul's Church; in 1952 Lancashire col-
lapsed from 125 for one to 141 all out.

But the match most remembered here was not a
county fixture but a local one, when Thornbury C.C.
met a scratch team. The year was 1902 and Thornbury's
captain was a sixty-two-year-old E. M. Grace. Perhaps
misguidedly, he put himself on to bowl when a certain
A. Hyman was in form. From two overs sixty-two
runs came, and by the time 100 minutes had passed Mr
Hyman had scored 359 runs, 192 of them coming in
sixes. It is a pity the sea is just too far away for it to have
featured in this dramatic innings, though one wonders
how many holidaymakers returned to Weston-super-
Mare in hope of seeing a repetition of such batting.

One of the delightful cast-iron supports to be seen at Clarence Park.

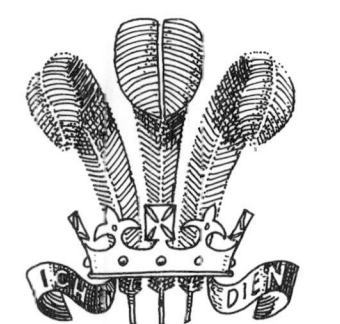

Surrey

Kennington Oval, London SE11 5SS

THE THIRD oldest of the county clubs, Surrey was formed in 1845, enjoying from the earliest possible time the status of first-class.

More than any other county, the ground has become indissolubly identified with the name, so that the Oval and Surrey are almost interchangeable. It is hardly surprising then that a comparison of home fixtures for the seasons spaced at half-century intervals shows no other ground until 1980 allows Guildford one match. The number of games played at the Oval is also interesting: 1880 had ten, 1930 nineteen, 1980 twelve.

The club colour is described as chocolate; and the emblem of the Prince of Wales' feathers signifies the association of the Oval with the Duchy of Cornwall.

THE OVAL

RIGHTLY has it been called 'The People's Ground', this pool of green in the desert of south-east London brick and asphalt. Here there is no atmosphere of leisured privilege, no Establishment, no aping of Lord's. For this is a ground confident of its own individuality, of its own setting, of its own honourable history.

There was a time when Kennington meant what it said: Kings town. Not more than 100 yards from the turnstiles one to five stood once a royal palace. Indeed in some ways this is more aristocratic ground than Lord's, for it is on land of the Duchy of Cornwall. In 1844 the Montpellier Club lost its ground, the Beehive, at Walworth. As a result, the following year saw the county club formed, and a former market garden become the Oval cricket ground. The score card of a match played on 13th May 1845 between the elevens of W. Fould and W. Houghton reveals that to a T. Phillips falls the dubious distinction being the first batsman to make an Oval duck.

The ground survived those early years though on one

occasion at least there had to be royal intervention, when the Prince Consort prevented the implementing of plans to build crescents of houses. Certainly the club must have been relieved when it finally secured the lease.

It is a great ground in more than one way, for in area it has pre-eminence. Indeed before there were fixed boundaries, when the wicket was pitched to one side of the table it was possible to run five. Its capacity is 20,000 of which 18,000 can be seated. Its hospitality is generous, for not only has it accommodated cricket but such activities as walking contests, poultry shows, football—even to having an F.A. Cup Final—'pop' festival, and a Sunday market at the Vauxhall end. It was here that the first Test Match in England took place in 1880, and here two years later that defeat by Australia which resulted in the Ashes.

By the last decade of the nineteenth century the pavilion and its adjacent nets stand had been built, with the west wing to follow; and the present Surrey Tavern, built twenty years ago, stands on the site of its 1897 predecessor. The pavilion must be the focus of interest for every visitor to the Oval. Its entrance hall has any number of score cards and a photocopy of the scorebook pages which recorded that Test Match of 1938 when England declared at 903 for seven, L. Hutton's contribution being 364. For those of us not fortunate enough to witness his historic innings, the voice of Howard Marshall on the radio serves as a reminder of that summer's day. What a match it was: Australia's defeat was by a record margin of an innings and 579 runs; rarely can Fleetwood-Smith's bowling read as one wicket for 298! Many years later, in 1951, Hutton again featured prominently in a Test Match here. This time it was against South Africa. In defending his wicket from a ball which had come off his bat or pad Hutton prevented Endean from making a catch, the umpire giving him out. P. B. H. May then came in, made a duck and returned to the pavilion so rapidly that D. C. S. Compton was quite unprepared, and was late going to the wicket. Despite all this, England won, interestingly the first victory at the Oval since that 1938 Test. May later redeemed his failure by scoring, against New Zealand, 165 which included a six that cleared the Vauxhall end.

There have been some great Test performances here. S. F. Barnes took 8 South African wickets for 20 runs in 1912; F. R. Spofforth had a match aggregate of 14 wickets for 90 in the 1882 'Ashes' match; G. L. Jessop scored a century in seventy-five minutes off the Australian bowlers in 1902; and in 1896 the Australian batsmen

The West wing at the Oval presents a classical face to the outside world.

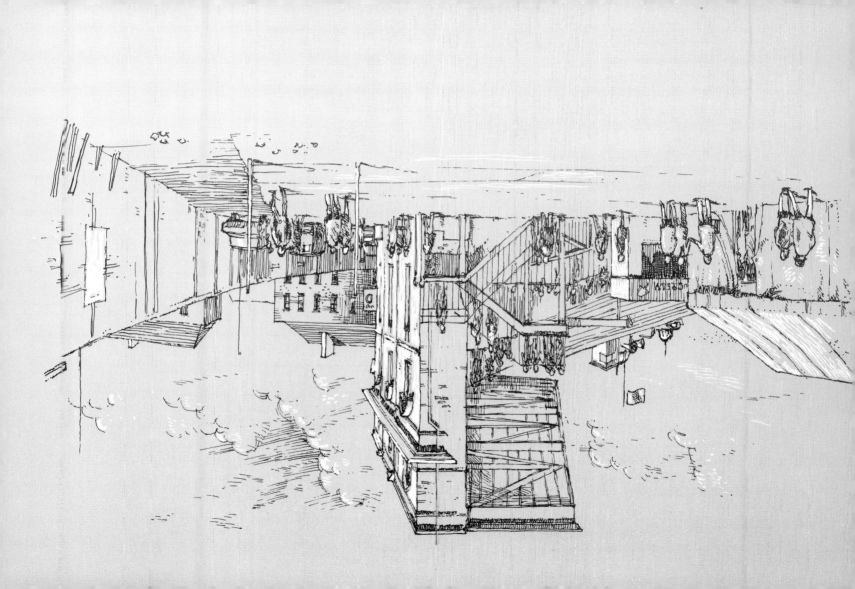

could accrue only forty-four between them. But in compensation it must be added that W. H. Ponsford and D. G. Bradman put on 451 for the second wicket in the 1934 Australian match.

However, this is above all Surrey's ground, and it is the county's records that deserve recounting. Here in 1899 the home side scored 811 against Somerset, R. Abel being undefeated with 357. In the same year Abel and T. Hayward had a fourth-wicket partnership of 448, though it should be noted that the visitors Yorkshire totalled 704.

The glory years of Surrey were surely those from 1952 to 1958 when the County Championship seemed permanently at the Oval. Matches like that against Warwickshire in 1953 which was over in a day, or that against Worcestershire the following year when twenty-five was the innings total of the visitors, of 'Laker's Match' in 1956 when he took all the Australian wickets in one innings for eighty-eight runs—these are some from those memorable years.

Of earlier seasons, H. A. Peach in 1924 took four Sussex wickets in four balls; in 1908 J. N. Crawford and F. C. Holland had a fifth wicket stand of 308, against Somerset; and in 1909 Hampshire bowlers conceded 742 runs, of which 371 were for the second wicket, the batsmen being E. G. Hayes and J. B. Hobbs.

How closely the Oval and Hobbs are associated, for it was not just his contribution to England, in the great opening partnerships with Sutcliffe that are remembered here, but also that long career with Surrey that began before the First World War. Then he was the cricketer in youthful exuberance, where strokes flowed from his bat with all the vigour and defiance of a man in his prime. After that war it was the maturity, the style, the classical ease that made him a model for all time. With 197 centuries in his career, six times a century in each innings of a match, sixteen centuries in the 1925 season, small wonder that it is Hobbs who is commemorated by the Main Gates erected in 1933.

In the pavilion Long Room, smart after its redecoration in 1978, many of these great personalities are remembered by paintings. Hobbs of course is there; so is A. Sandham, his partner so many times, and never more so than in that of 428 against Oxford University in 1926; the patriarchal W. E. Roller, going in to bat with tie, H. Leveson-Gower, Henry Marshall, Surridge, the members and players.

The Long Room at the Oval has all the dignity one expects at a major ground.

The Oval from the scorebox. [following pages]

The display cases have a wealth of interest, for the historian: that bat of 1726 must be the grandfather of them all. There are the memorials to those who fell in the World Wars, and the almost obligatory bust of W. G. Grace. Photographs of past teams abound in the Members' bar, while on the stairs those famous cartoons by 'Spy' have more than decorative appeal, for it was that of Spofforth who destroyed the English batting here in 1882 which set the fashion for these lithographs in *Vanity Fair*.

Few grounds can retain so well the character of London as the Oval. Massive arched windows in the brick and stone pavilion, the turrets bearing great trumpets, the iron awnings over the balcony, that centre flagmast reserved for the royal standard—and let it not be forgotten that since 1905 the club has proudly used the Prince of Wales' feathers—the oddly-shaped west wing looking from the end like part of the Colosseum—these give the south side of the ground a richness and variety belied by the intimidating perimeter wall that in its shape gives the ground its name.

But climb to the top of the pavilion and look north.

It is not difficult to see a similarity between the pavilion here at the Oval and that at Old Trafford, for they were designed by the same architect.

what a panorama of London presents itself. Other
grounds may have their hills, trees or cathedrals to
enjoy, here there is the backcloth of a great city.

On the left Archbishop Tenison's Grammar School
with its sober Georgian-style façade has as neighbours
two blocks of flats named Stoddart and Shrewsbury;
strange they should be two England batsmen who were
not Surrey players, and even more tragic that they both
committed suicide! Further north, Harleyford Road
leads the eye on to the banded tower of Westminster
Cathedral. Tower blocks of more recent date rear
beyond the Vauxhall stand, the dominant surely being
Millbank's. Those encircling flats now begin to change
from anonymous twentieth-century Georgian to
warmer Victorian, their pedimented windows and
parapet roofs bringing a pleasant reminder of how much
of this scene would have looked once. Behind them
stand the celebrated gas holders. At least one bowler has
found their presence useful: A. Gover, that great fast
bowler, preferred to work down-wind, so his first job
was to decide which end he would use by the smell of
either brewery or gasworks. Originally there were five,
but one was demolished recently. They vary in date
from 1850 to 1955, and in diameter from 138 to 214 feet,

Inside the main scoreboard at the Oval: the successor to that of 1848.

the largest, completed in 1877 having a capacity of over 5½ million cubic feet. Through their latticework the Houses of Parliament and the Post Office Tower can be seen. The broad sweep of the east terrace has the 'Cricketers' roof, with its dormers, behind, and then further flats bring the eye round to the new Mound stand.

During the Second World War the Oval was prepared for a very different role, that of a camp to receive prisoners. In the event it was not used, but that did not mean restoration was easy afterwards. Indeed the turf had to be relaid and extensive damage from shrapnel made good.

Today plans are to develop the Vauxhall end. The sum needed for a sports centre is over £2 million. It is typical of the Oval that, having never had a practice ground, nor even a car park, it should envisage this plan as serving the local community as much as county or Test players.

For though it may be no longer the case that a ball might land on an open-top omnibus, the Oval remains essentially part of South-east London. Maybe the cockney comments from the terrace are echoed everywhere today, but no other ground has so captured the affection of its neighbours.

And if you feel that cricket has been left behind, take a walk along nearby Belgrave Road. It will not be long before you come to hotels named Hammond's, Hutton's and, naturally, Hobbs'!

Sussex

County Ground, Eaton Road, Hove, BN3 3AN

THE CLUB, one of the oldest amongst the counties, was founded in 1839. As the opponent of Kent in the only match of that abortive County Cup competition of 1873 it can claim a history of first-class status as long as any other.

Certainly the 1880 season's matches are exceeded in number only by Surrey's, but Sussex has the superiority in meeting the Australians, and in using two grounds: Hastings as well as Hove. By 1930 Eastbourne and Horsham have been added. The 1980 season shows that Hove has established itself as the main venue, with nine matches, including the Tourists', Eastbourne having its Week of two matches, and Hastings but one.

The club colours are appropriate for this county with so long a coast: dark and light blue and gold. Six martlets form the emblem, and they are one of the more puzzling birds of heraldry. Because the swallow rarely is seen except on the wing the idea grew that no feet were necessary, and thus the martlet came into existence. Whether a pun on the French *l'hirondelle* refers to Arundel—itself associated with cricket through the Duke of Norfolk's matches there—or whether, as has been suggested, an early sheriff of Sussex used it to denote he had no lands must remain conjecture.

HOVE

WHAT kind of place is promised by 'the County Ground, Hove'? Is it going to be lined by gracious Regency houses with perhaps a hint of sharawaggi; will it have glorious views of the Downs or broad sweeps of the sea; is there a pavilion, ornate and impressive in its Victorian style boasting cast-iron balcony and picture-filled Long Room; will the entrance gates have some famous son of Sussex commemorated on the massive piers; or, will it be little more than a recreation ground with a puny pavilion accompanied by some rustic stand, its seating augmented by deck chairs; is the background going to be intimidating offices, or blocks of seaside flats? What will its character be: friendly, fashionable or flibbertigibbet? Turn off that motorway of an esplanade called Kingsway, along the Drive till Eaton Road reveals the entrance to the county ground. Then these questions will be answered, and in a strange way most of them in the affirmative.

Yes, there are Memorial Gates: to Tate. But which one? For this will be a timely reminder that Sussex has had a tradition of family cricket, and the Tates, father and son, are the first of many examples at Hove. F. W. or Fred, began his career in 1887. A fast bowler who took 1,341 wickets, his great performance here must include 9 for 24, against Hampshire, and 7 for 7 against Oxford University, both in 1891. In five seasons he took over 100 wickets, and in 1902 he was chosen to play for England in the Test Match at Old Trafford. Never was an appearance so tragic for in Australia's second innings he dropped a catch that resulted in the Tourists winning by four runs, and it was his wicket that was the last to fall when he had hit four of the eight needed. His only consolation was expressed in "I've got a little kid at home there who'll make up for it to me". Maurice was then seven years old, but he justified that hope. In eight seasons from 1922 to 1929 he secured the 'double', and at Hove he once scored 203, in a second wicket partnership of 385 with E. H. Bowley. He took ten or more wickets in a match thirty-seven times, and five or more in an innings 151 times; in four consecutive seasons he totalled 799 wickets. No wonder it is M. W. Tate who has become the synonym for all pace-bowlers. The gates may not be as ostentatious as those at Lords, but the hotel next to them would be acceptable there, or indeed at Trent Bridge. It is now called the 'Sussex Cricketer' but its original name County Cricket Ground Hotel can still be identified, and how redolent of the place it sounds.

Beyond the lawn and rose bushes the line of buildings stretches due north, to form one side of the field, a field which seems to climb even more than its ten feet. First comes the secretary's office, originally the professionals' changing-rooms. Next is the Wilbury stand, including the scorebox and Press, together with scoreboard and its reminder of 'Ranji', for in 1934 reconstruction was carried out in his memory. What better way of marking that elegant batsman's feat here in scoring two separate centuries in one day? K. S. Ranjitsinhji, or to give him his full title H. H. the Jam Sahib of Nawanager, played for the county in twelve seasons, during which he accrued 18,594 runs. The first to score over 3,000 in a

The pavilion Long Room at Hove.

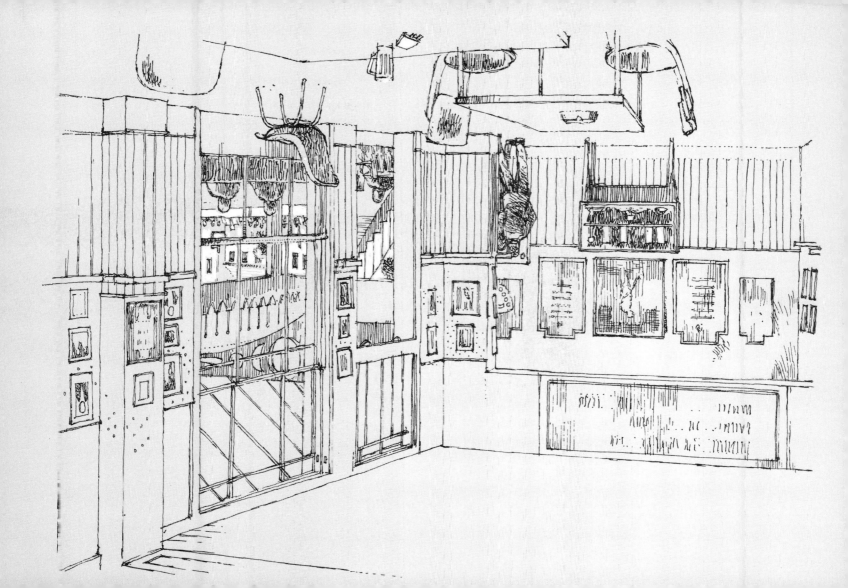

season, on three occasions he needed only one month to total 1,000.

Once again, family ties emerge: Ranji's nephew was Duleepsinhji, who also captained the XI, and, like his uncle, scored a century in his first Test Match against Australia. In 1930 he made 333 in one day, here.

The pavilion at Hove is hard to find, for, since the rebuilding at the beginning of the 1960s, its exterior has been so thoroughly integrated with the next stand—before equality known as the Ladies stand—that only a somewhat diminutive clock and low roof reveals its identity. Inside, with its 1978 extension, there is a wealth of history on the walls.

Painted portraits include many great personalities of Sussex cricket. To many students of the cinema Sir C. Aubrey Smith is remembered as an Elgar-like actor often cast as an irascible colonel or duke, but to Hove he is a past captain, nicknamed 'round-the-corner-Smith' because of his unusual run-up and round arm action, a man who went with English teams to South Africa and Australia, who took cricket to Hollywood and played till he was eighty-three.

G. R. Cox is also there: a bowler who took 1,810 wickets in a career that saw him still active at fifty-three. Note that his son G. appears too, in the portrait photographs, for he was a batsman of no mean ability as his 234 not out against India here in 1946 demonstrates.

A further portrait, of A. E. R. Gilligan, illustrates better than any other that family characteristic of Sussex. The stand at the sea end of the ground with its indoor school was named after him, and one wonders why the club waited till 1972 to perpetuate the name at Hove. For here was a career that began in 1920, included the captaincy of the county side, formed a partnership with M. Tate that was the envy and fear of other counties—and countries, for did not these two bowl out South Africa in 1924 for thirty runs—Chairman and President.

His brother A. H. H. also captained the XI, and was involved in an unusual 'dismissal' here in 1919 when, thinking he was bowled, he walked from the crease; whereupon the Lancashire wicket-keeper removed the bails. But at the close of the innings the square-leg umpire ruled he was not stumped. So his dismissal remains a mystery to this day. Incidentally another brother, F. W., captained Essex, though unlike the others he did not captain an M.C.C. tour.

Other mementoes attract the visitor: there is Ranji's blazer bearing his family motto on the badge, a sweater worn by C. B. Fry during the season he scored six consecutive centuries, wicket-keeping gloves used by Harry Phillips, the first player to dispense with a long stop, and bats, scorecards printed on silk, and any number of photographs.

Fascinating as these exhibits are, and nearby there is a growing library that puts many other counties to shame, it is the ground which demands some further words. The north end has grass terraces allowing that characteristic array of deck chairs which is repeated down by the Gilligan stand. Behind rises one of the massive blocks of flats which dwarf even the substantial houses lining the north and east sides.

It is on this latter side that the Harmsworth scoreboard of 1930 patriarchally presides, its imperial top looking more suited to Lord's. Next to it impudently sits what is known as the 'hen-run' or 'chicken-coop': at one time it served as the ladies' pavilion on the northwest, but was moved here, doubtless to be nearer the other rustic stand called the 'cow shed' that occupied the south end.

This ground is the fourth used by Sussex, a club which began in 1839. The Prince Regent gave it the first, Ireland's Gardens, after which came the Montpellier and Royal Brunswick grounds. In 1872, after the last crop of barley had been harvested and the 20-foot slope reduced, the first county match took place, with Gloucestershire. Heavy rain prevented its finishing, though the crowd

Hove's professionals had their changing-rooms in what are now the administration offices.

did see W. G. Grace lose his wicket for the third time in as many days to bowler Southerton. The weather since then has contributed its fair share of sunshine, showers and sea mist.

Here, not only have the great names of Sussex—the Gilligans, Langridges, Parkses, Oakses, Tates, one must stop—played, but others too have appeared: Amy Johnson, back from one of her record-breaking flights, came to meet Don Bradman during an extended tea interval. Is this the only county ground to have had a game interrupted by an aircraft dropping a bomb? Fortunately the addition to the field did not explode. And it was the Yorkshire match that was the only one of the County Championship in progress when war was declared in 1939: Sussex were bowled out for thirty-three by H. Verity who, having given his county the Championship, bade farewell to cricket for he was killed in Italy on active service.

Today the ground looks very different from what it was in 1872. The last of the blocks of flats has been finished on the south side; the patronage has changed, witness the advertisements on the covers; the cricket is more intensive.

Yet in other ways Hove stays the same: the same clarity of light, the same freshness, the same enthusiasm for the game, and the same view of the sea—just.

EASTBOURNE

MANY grounds have beautiful settings and dull names; others compensate for the ordinariness of the first by the fullsome second. But with the Saffrons at Eastbourne both aspects seem to be favoured.

Dominated on the east side by the towers and spires of the town, and on the west by Compton Place Park with the Sussex hills beyond, it is a delight to visit. Although there are many trees visible, the attractiveness here lies in the association of many different components: trees, yes, but also brick and flint, rich tiles and smart wood, all bathed in that bright light only a seaside place seems to be able to provide.

This is a private ground; although a football pitch may be evident, and there are two hockey pitches each end of the cricket table, the stamp of the Devonshire family can be sensed. For the Eastbourne Club which plays here has had many grounds in the town, the immediate predecessor being Devonshire Park, a gift of the Duke.

However in 1884 cricket moved to the Saffrons, the name originating from the previous use of the land for

The impressive Town Hall, and church spires dominate the Saffrons ground at Eastbourne.

that orange-yellow species of crocus grown for dyeing and medical purposes. Quite soon expenditure was authorised for the purchase of another horse to pull the mower and roller, at a cost not exceeding £10; and cricket balls at no more than £3 a dozen.

The main pavilion on the west side of the ground replaces one destroyed by fire in 1947, being rebuilt in 1960 and reconstructed in 1978. It could not be considered of great beauty or interest but its variety of roofs and its mixture of materials give it a certain character.

From its terrace the fine skyline of those towers rising above the football stand and trees can best be enjoyed. The elaborate domed top of the Town Hall catches the eye first, as indeed it should, for it displays the clock that the umpires go by! Both ground and town hall are the same age, 1884, while the spire of SS Saviours and Peter, on the far right, is seventeen years older being the work of that great architect of the London Law Courts, G. E. Street. Between them stands the Roman Catholic church of 1901.

On the south side, or Meads Road end, the First World War Memorial pavilion built of red brick has the squash courts adjoining, while further east is the Harry Bartlett pavilion—they go in for pavilions at the Saffrons.

During the Festival of course, there are tents and marquees, some private, others for the public to use. Temporary stands fill the rest of the boundary so that the football terraces are hidden behind them and the cars that use the pitch.

North of the scoreboard, beyond the tents and trees more cars are parked in Larkin's Field, named after a saddler who in the eighteenth century grazed his cattle there. Maybe it now should be Fletcher's Field as archery is practised from time to time.

The Saffrons has had the reputation of being a batsman's ground, perhaps the light has had something to do with it. Certainly there have been some memorable innings by individuals. In 1901 C. B. Fry scored 219 not out against Oxford University; R. R. Relf, one of three brothers who played for Sussex, achieved the highest innings of his career here when he was undefeated with 272 in the Worcestershire match of 1909, and in 1920 followed this with 225 against Lancashire. J. Langridge scored 215 off Glamorgan in 1938, and 1948 saw H. Gimblett of Somerset achieve no less than 310.

What a pity that J. B. Hobbs appeared here only once, and D. Bradman never had the opportunity of a visit. Doubtless he would have relished the chance to avenge that match of 1921.

This was a match that the Australians wanted to win, for up till then their season had been twenty wins and fourteen draws. Having won the Test rubber they now wanted to be the first Tourists to return undefeated. Their opponents here were A. C. MacLaren's XI, a team composed entirely of amateurs, who, in their first innings, made only 43 and that on a perfect wicket. The Australians replied with 174. In their second innings after being 60 for 4, MacLaren's men recovered to reach 326. All the Tourists needed was 196. By lunch on the last day they were 109 and five wickets standing. When they were 140, their nerve failed, and the innings ended with them twenty-eight runs short.

The crowd went wild with excitement. Armstrong the Australian captain made a sportsmanlike speech declaring his men had been beaten by the better side. But MacLaren did not appear, some saying he was too over-come by emotion. For this was his last first-class match and he had done what nobody thought was possible.

What better place than the Saffrons for so remarkable a victory?

Warwickshire

County Ground, Edgbaston, Birmingham B5 7QU

A RELATIVE late-comer to the cricket counties, Warwickshire's club was formed in 1884, and eleven years later became first-class.

Like the other counties with Test Match grounds, the overwhelming majority of home matches have been centred on Edgbaston: in 1930 thirteen, in 1980 ten, with only Nuneaton and Coventry able to wrest one game each.

Blue, gold and silver are the club colours. The emblem is the badge of the Beauchamp family, the famous bear and ragged staff. When it passed to Nevill, Earl of Warwick, its adoption by the county was but a matter of time, and today its presence extends from that on sweaters to the weather-vane on Edgbaston's scoreboard.

BIRMINGHAM

OFF THE spacious Pershore Road, in a part of Birmingham that has such things as the BBC television centre, you will find the Edgbaston Cricket Ground. Indeed it is spelled out in generous letters across the façade of the west wing, lest you mistake it for another television centre or some magnificent exhibition.

Here is a splendid site, seemingly limitless in its extent and sparkling in its apparent newness: to the south Cannon Hill Park, to the north Calthorpe Park, to the east the River Rea, though in fact there is the Colts' ground, with a car park, on the further side.

Through the Thwaite Gates, their piers proudly surmounted by the bear-and-ragged-staff of Warwickshire, a different aspect presents itself. Now there are bright flowers, roses and trellis work, grass, cafe tables with sun shades creating almost a Continental scene. To the left, gently curving away is a towering wall of glass, concrete, and brick, like some modern counterpart of Regent Street. At ground level coloured awnings appear to shade shop fronts, while above generous windows seem to be intended for diners. To the right more concrete and glass stretch, past shrubs till the boundary wall almost closes the view.

Improbable as it may seem you are looking at the backs of the William Ansell stand and the pavilion west wing. If you then examine carefully the gap between them, under the smart railed walkway it should be possible to detect a cricket field.

What may prove a little more difficult will be to spot the pavilion, for its original shape is almost obliterated by so many subsequent additions that if it were not for a steep pitched tiled roof bearing a tiny spirelet the task would be beyond any but the most observant.

And it is little easier from the field, for the most conspicuous indeed almost dominant building is that scoreboard on the opposite side. Like the entrance gates it commemorates Dr Harold Thwaite, one of those personalities who are as essential to a county club as the great players, I mean the officials who, often unpaid, give their talents in ensuring sound administration and financial stability. The scoreboard is perhaps the most recognisable of any on the first-class grounds: the doll's-

The back of Edgbaston's pavilion illustrates well the changes that have been made over the years.

house proportions, the pantiled roof ending in elegant hips, a weather-vane with the Warwick bear, and a gable for the clock that could have come from Amsterdam. It is not only its shape but its brilliant contrasts of black and white which attract the eye.

All round the ground vast concrete terraces make their low gradients against contrary motion stand-roofs. On the west side particularly the sheer extent of the tiers gives the feeling of an amphitheatre of Olympian scale.

More homely, and more interesting in their façades are the Hill Bank stands near the scoreboard, the Press box and its companion bringing just the right touch of informality. From the sightscreen block, the Stanley Barnes stand, or indeed any of the seating the scoreboard end, a fine view can be enjoyed, not only of the immaculate field, nor just the widespread pavilion wings, but also of the Chamberlain tower of the University, church spires, massive blocks of flats, and a row of poplars which seems to never end.

Behind, the great city stretches northward to the more distant horizon, a skyline of Birmingham's new architecture that offers examples to identify however hazy the weather—or the knowledge.

A sound knowledge of Warwickshire cricket is expected of those walking round Edgbaston; for you will discover that names of past officers are liberally used—William Ansell, secretary 1882 to 1902, Baron Cal-thorpe, president 1907, Dr Stanley Barnes, president 1955, and of course Dr Harold Thwaite, secretary 1941, president 1943 to 1955. You will also find it useful to know the positions of fine leg, third man, extra cover, gully and long off if you need refreshment, for these are the names given to the bars.

Past players too are remembered, and nowhere more appropriately than in the pavilion's club room. Here in an atmosphere of carpeted and upholstered comfort with the large windows looking out across the field, you may (if you are a male) examine at leisure the portrait gallery of players, presidents. Team photographs abound both here and in the players' dining-room. There are bats and balls, each one recalling a fine cricketer or a memorable match performance.

One unusual item is a fan of 1911 signed by the players in the match at the Oval between the Champion County of that season and the Rest. Need it be added that the County was Warwickshire? The previous year bottom-but-two had been its place, but in 1911 under the captaincy of F. R. Foster—whose year it must have been, beginning with that Test in Australia when he took 5 wickets for 36 runs—the side upset all the predictions of the experts. In that Eleven the wicket-keeper was

Looking south to the pavilion from the press box stand at Edgbaston.

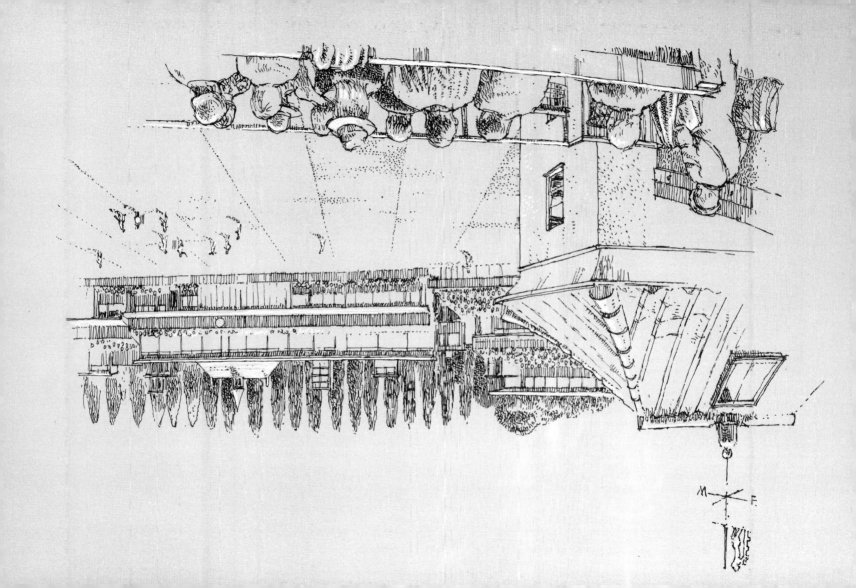

E. J. (Tiger) Smith. He too went to Australia in that Ashes-winning tour, and perhaps his greatest match was here at Edgbaston in 1926 against Derbyshire when he became the first to dismiss seven batsmen in an innings. That was not his only record, for he saved the other to the end: when he died at ninety-three in 1979 he was the oldest Test cricketer, outliving his exact contemporary F. E. Woolley by a year.

The club room has many other mementoes of Warwickshire cricket, and the displays are varied enough to make it difficult to single out special items, but surely mention must be made of M. J. K. Smith's spectacles, the pair he wore throughout the 1959 season.

How many names appear in this pavilion, which has seen virtually the whole history of the club, from its formation in 1884, its first match in 1886 against the M.C.C., its first county match with Nottinghamshire in 1894; it has seen that mammoth 387 made by Yorkshire in 1896, and the century that C. M. Old achieved for that county in 1977—when many a member might

Edgbaston's comfortable Club Room displays many mementoes of Warwickshire cricket, as well as affording a fine view of the game.

The Sydney Barnes memorial gate in the forecourt of Edgbaston.

have missed it, for it took only thirty-seven minutes, with the second fifty coming in but nine! It has seen Hampshire shot out for 15 in 1922, and it has witnessed an unbroken stand of 465 for the second wicket between J. A. Jameson and R. E. Kanhai in the 1974 Gloucestershire match.

There have been Test Matches here since 1902, though after 1929, for some thirty-five years, there were none. Nevertheless Edgbaston has been the scene of such performances other grounds, fortunate to have had more international cricket, would be proud of.

In that first year the Tourists were Australian and they did not relish the visit, thirty-six being their innings total. It was the Yorkshireman W. Rhodes whose slow left-arm bowling took 7 wickets for 17 runs. In 1924 South Africa was also humbled here with an innings that could manage only 30, with the highest score being the eleven extras.

But for bowling endurance surely S. Ramadhin's must rank high: in the 1957 West Indies Test his match deliveries were 774, 588 being in the first innings.

The dominating feature of Edgbaston is its scoreboard, and its interior is no less impressive. It is interesting to recall that before such a facility was available to players and spectators, the only indication of the state of play was the scorers standing up when the totals were level.

However, they were gratefully received by the Surrey batsman P. B. H. May who scored 285 not out.

Edgbaston has been host to teams of all kinds, even international hockey has been played. It is now one of the major cricket grounds of England, imposing and expansive, a place anyone would feel honoured to play at.

How good therefore to find a small archway in the boundary wall designated "the Sydney Barnes wicket-gate", in being "the point where he entered the ground on 20th August 1894 to play in the first county match, and where his ashes now rest".

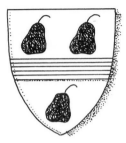

Worcestershire

County Ground, New Road, Worcester WR2 4QQ

THIS county shares the distinction with Derbyshire, in that both clubs having achieved first-class status, relinquished it temporarily. In the case of Worcestershire it was for but one year, 1919, exactly twenty years after becoming a member of the Championship. Interestingly, the club despite having been founded in 1865 does not appear to have been included in the categories of the 1890 County Cricket Council.

Nevertheless the records of the 1930 season show as full a programme of first-class matches as most: fifteen played, Worcester itself having ten, including as by tradition the first match with the Australians, Kiddermin-ster three, Dudley and Stourbridge each one. In 1980 eleven are at Worcester and one at Stourport-on-Severn.

The club colours are sombre: dark green and black, the latter echoing the rich Worcester pears on the emblem.

WORCESTER

OPEN a book of colour photographs depicting 'the face of Britain', check the sport pages of newspapers at the beginning of the cricket season, ask almost anybody to suggest the most beautiful county ground, and the chances are that in each case Worcester will be the choice.

It is the view across the ground to the cathedral on the other bank of the River Severn that has the greatest appeal, and so dominant a feature deserves a description.

Unquestionably the building makes a fine, perhaps even superb, sight. The 196-foot high central tower, pinnacled and richly carved, rises behind the great west window flanked by its own pinnacles. Such a majestic display of gothic architecture is best seen from a distance, for though the tower be fourteenth century, it must be admitted that the west window dates only from 1865.

However the cathedral has had more than just a visual association with the county ground. When the cricket club was formed in 1865 it used Boughton Park, and for a few years it served reasonably well, indeed by 1872 a Cricket Week was proposed and matches were arranged with the Free Foresters and M.C.C. However, when, following its overwhelming superiority in winning the Minor Counties Competition three years in succession, Worcestershire became a first-class county in 1899 a move had been made to land owned by the Dean and Chapter of the cathedral.

Perhaps the persistence of a pastoral atmosphere at New Road is explained by the fact that the cathedral's land was a farm, and on more than one occasion the tenant farmer who had had to sacrifice three of his fields was known to allow his stock the freedom of the ground.

The club had enthusiastic officials and players who ensured that the first county match would not find the setting unworthy on the day. Thus it was that the morning of 4th May 1899 saw the honorary secretary painting the sightscreens before the teams emerged from the new pavilion, itself only just completed.

Few grounds have so delightful a pavilion balcony as Worcester's; note the weather-vane, too.

Yorkshire was the visiting side, and although there was every likelihood of a defeat for the home side, the margin was only eleven runs, thanks to a fine spell of bowling by G. Wilson. He took eight of the Champions' wickets for seventy runs, so that Worcestershire led by seventy-two on the first innings.

Naturally enough, for was not the county nicknamed' 'Fostershire', the three Foster brothers played in that match, H. K. as captain. Seven brothers eventually played for the club, but the most famous was R. E. who held the record for the highest Test score made by an English batsman in Australia.

If the cathedral has the greatest visual influence, the river has the greatest physical. Look closely at the buildings around the boundary and it will be clear what that influence is, for they are all on stilts! Although the leg-pull may be that the heavy roller has to be anchored, it is nevertheless incontrovertible that this ground is frequently flooded. A plate in the pavilion records the 1947 water level, and it is as high as the windows. Fred Hunt, that Kent player, who became the first groundsman once caught a 45-pound salmon, and moreover also asserted that he had found the heavy roller upside down two fields away.

Despite the floods the delightful pavilion has survived. It is a pity that the ornate woodwork and the charming weather-vane never appear in those stock photographs, for many a ground would be glad to possess so fine an example of cricket architecture dating from the turn of the century. How good to see it so well looked after.

Indeed the whole ground positively sparkles with freshness and light. The paintwork gleams white against the rich green of the superb turf – what turf it is too. Why, in the 1920s they used to play bowls on the southwest outfield, after matches were over for the day; and in 1964 a tennis tournament was held there.

Apart from the pavilion most of the building has taken place since 1952. In that year the ladies' pavilion, the dining-room and offices, and scoreboard were provided; the press box, the terrace and Severn bar came in 1967; while the New Road stand had to wait till 1974.

Improvements have not been confined to buildings, though. Trees are so much a feature of this ground, from any position around the boundary it is certain that the play will have luxuriant foliage as its background. On the east side a fine copper beech has been planted, Don

A scene not uncommon at Worcester.

The magnificent panorama at Worcester, from the pavilion. [following pages]

Kenyon's tree, and on the south-west near the ladies' pavilion a Worcester black pear at last has a place, for that is the fruit represented on the club's badge.

Since 1976 the ground has been owned by the Club and those perilous years, when it seemed first-class cricket might not be seen at New Road the next season, are but an unpleasant memory.

Three times the County Championship has come to Worcester and the record in other competitions is a credit to the smallest cricket county.

There is one other reason for this ground securing a regular place in the newspaper sports pages each season: since the 1920s it has been the custom for the Touring sides to begin their round of County games here. The Australians' visit in 1930 was memorable not only because they scored 423 runs, but also that a young batsman named D. Bradman made 236 of them in four-and-a-half hours. His second appearance here was in 1934, when 206 was his personal contribution, 1938 saw him relish the occasion to the tune of 258. However his next visit was a relative failure, for he made only 148!

Another touring side, South Africa, came here in 1901, when the match was notable not for high scoring but for the last man being stumped with the scores level.

Nevertheless, this ground has seen some mighty innings. The Warwickshire match of 1906 was remarkable for a total of 633; the Leicestershire game in the same year even more with the visitors losing only four wickets in scoring 701. In the Gloucestershire game of 1933 two batsmen, Dacre and Hammond, completed centuries in both innings, repeating the performance of W. L. and R. E. Foster who had achieved the same against Hampshire in 1899.

If the Foster brothers returned to New Road today the view from the pavilion steps would be familiar to them. The panorama still takes in the tower of All Saints, with St Nicholas' eighteenth-century lantern-top beyond. They would recognise the hop warehouse to the right, and the elegant spire of St Andrews. The copper cupola of the Police Headquarters would be unfamiliar as it was not placed there till 1941, while the 1960 technical college mercifully is partially hidden by trees. Its neighbour is the thirteenth-century bishops' palace, with a fine seventeenth-century house between it and the cathedral. Next comes the wide-splayed roof line of the refectory, and then, behind the hunchback half-timbered scoreboard, the red brick buildings of the King's School. Away to the right, beyond the sightscreen amongst distant trees rises the majestic outline of what to the Fosters might have been Townsend's flour mills, today it is the Royal Worcester Porcelain Works. Still the carillon rings out from the cathedral tower at midday, 3 o'clock and 6 o'clock.

Such is that view, breathtaking in its beauty on a

summer's evening when the westerly sunshine lights up the stonework and the trees. Maybe Worcester's danger is in prettying too much its ground: already there are flower-tubs on the roof of the Severn bar, and 'sponsored flowers' in the pavilion enclosure. The club has far too much sense than to overdo these matters, for it knows what a 'goodly heritage' it possesses at New Road.

Yorkshire

Headingley Cricket Ground, Leeds LS6 3BW

THE CLUB was formed in 1863, and like eight other counties it can date its designation as first–class back to 1873.

In the 1880 season the overwhelmingly majority of its home fixtures were at Sheffield, with Huddersfield having but two, and only Scarborough featuring at the end with a match against I Zingari. By 1930 the pattern had changed to the characteristic spread of grounds. Sheffield had five matches including the Australian; Bradford four, also having the Australians; Leeds had three; Dewsbury, Harrogate, Hull and Scarborough each one. And of course there was a Test Match at Leeds.

In 1980 the range of grounds has only marginally decreased: Leeds three matches; Sheffield two; Bradford three; Middlesbrough one; Harrogate one; Scarborough two, together with Festival matches. And again a Test Match takes place at Leeds.

The club colours are the same as those of Sussex, dark and light blue, and gold, but there is no likelihood of confusion over the emblems, for what else could the club have other than the white rose of York?

LEEDS

HEADINGLEY is a name as well-known as Old Trafford or Trent Bridge for it also is a Test Match ground. Like them it has taken its title from the suburb of the city where space was available. In the case of Leeds, Headingley came onto the market as part of the Cardigan Fields estate in 1888, as 'Lot 17a'.

From such anonymous a beginning, the ground rapidly developed under its new owner, the Leeds Cricket Football and Athletic Co. Ltd. As the name implies there has always been a multiplicity of use, and indeed this must be considered one of the important characteristics of Headingley.

Another is the fact that the county club does not own

the ground, which is not quite the same thing as its having the lease: in this respect it differs from the Oval, but in a way is comparable with Middlesex at Lord's.

For those reasons alone Headingley is a unique place, unmistakable in its appearance and highly individual in character.

A further strange facet is the absence of a reference point in respect of the wicket. The usual arrangement is for the pavilion to be facing down the pitch or to be parallel to it, but here the location, let alone the identity of such a building is a source of some doubt.

What the batsman at the north, or Kirkstall Lane end, faces is the massive bulk of the main stand, a structure and name that is ambivalent for it could be said that it owes its existence to the football field on the south. Certainly the seating for cricket watching seems to be there as an afterthought. On Good Friday 1932, its predecessor was burned down, and at a cost of £20,000 this took its place. Here are located the commentary and Press boxes, with the television cameras above. So at least there is no need for unsightly scaffolding or precariously perched sheds.

At the south-east corner of the ground, next to the main stand, is to be found the building that most closely fills the role of a pavilion. Indeed it merits the name of old pavilion, and in its original form it had all the conventional character of one. There was a high centre with generous balcony, capped by a steep pitched roof carrying the cupola, while the wings had their own tiled gables and chimney stacks. The similarity with Trent Bridge was marked.

But today you will see a very different place. Gone is the centre, and instead rises an 'airport terminal' its white concrete façade capped by a roof of green copper. To one side a tower ends in a clock turret of such puny proportions that you wonder the umpires bother to use it. All that remain externally as reminder of the old pavilion are the wings. A featureless balcony stretches interminably from one side to the other, looking more appropriate on the sun deck of some ocean-liner—except that here the spectators are facing north.

The new pavilion is on the more easterly perimeter. A long low building, it has all the fragility of a matchbox. Doubtless it is very convenient and well-appointed, but no connoisseur of cricket fields could pronounce it worthy of a major ground. Perhaps I am being harsh, for in truth it does not call itself a pavilion, merely offices and dressing-rooms. Yet it is from here that the players emerge, and to it the batsman who has completed his century returns. There are few who support the back-

---

Headingley, from the West Terrace, looking across to the County Club' offices and dressing-rooms. [following pages]

slapping which can make such a return a greater ordeal than the 'bouncers', but there is equally something very unsatisfactory about that walk past the square-leg umpire to a building bereft of members. Instead of disappearing into the mystery of Long Room, there has to be a little jump up on to the terrace, then two flights of exposed stairs to climb and a walk along a balcony before the haven of a dressing-room. Granted that in less ostentatious days a batsman who made a century would modestly run back to the pavilion, but the unfortunate maker of a duck today dare not copy that, even at Headingley.

On the north and west sides of the ground great expanses of terraces sweep round. Directly behind the bowler's arm is the famous 'chad stand', so called because the rows of disembodied heads of spectators above the white boards are reminiscent of that once ubiquitous cartoon deliverer of pertinent observations beginning, "Wot, no . . . ?"

Beyond the Winter Shed stand and the scoreboard is the line of poplars, planted, it is said, to prevent free viewing from outside the ground. There are thirty now, but it is doubtful if they will ever completely achieve the aim. For one thing, the houses that gently climb the hill to the graceful spire of St Michael and All Angels have very sensibly introduced generous dormer windows!

On Test Match days it is a fine sight for those in Cardigan Road or St Michaels Lane. The luncheon marquees are pitched on that spacious lawn by the Sutcliffe Gates, flags fly from the staffs on the main stand and the pavilion, and the whole occasion is made memorable for the crowds coming up from the city. The impeccable grass looks even greener because of the crisp edge of kerb and asphalt—the 'athletic' bit of the company included cycling.

And before long Yorkshire voices are working hard. They will tell of 'Roses' matches, of Holmes and Sutcliffe, Hutton and Rhodes, Emmett and Leyland, Jackson, Verity, Bowes . . . what partnerships, what personalities, inexhaustible in variety and indeed almost in number.

Those matches when the omnipotence of Yorkshire batting seemed unquestioned: 1921 against Leicestershire, 560 for 6 declared; 1925 against Middlesex, 528 for 6 declared; 1953 against Somerset 525 for 4 declared; when the skill of her bowlers was overwhelming: 1902, Australia 23; 1906 Leicestershire 34; 1904, Hampshire, 36.

And the memorable Test Matches that have been witnessed here will be also recounted by those old enough

The Members' stand and the 'pavilion' lead to the Main Stand that is the back of the Football Field stand.

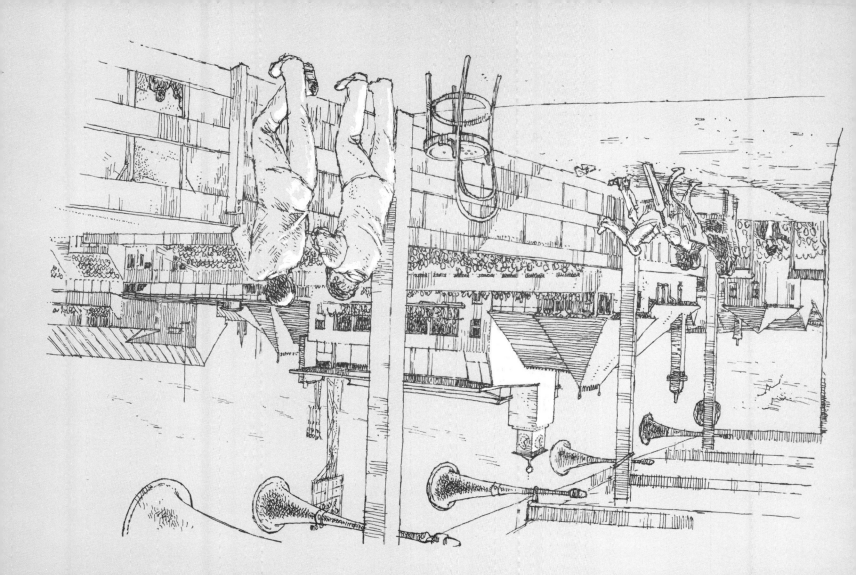

to have been present. Some may remember 1930 when Australia made 458 for 3 on the first day, Bradman scoring 105 before lunch and 115 between lunch and tea, eventually accumulating 334; or that repetition four years later with the second day scoreboard showing 455 for one—interestingly Bradman eventually made 304 and Ponsford 181, but nobody else had a score higher than 27. More will recall the 1948 Test when the total runs for 31 wickets reached the colossal 1723. Others may prefer to forget the 1955 Test against South Africa when T. E. Bailey took two hours to score eight runs. And, of course, every Yorkshireman will quickly tell you that it was here in 1977 that G. Boycott became the first player to complete a century of centuries in a Test Match.

The Third Test against Australia in 1961 was played here on a pitch that some condemned as not fit for anything resembling cricket. That F. Trueman took 6 wickets for 5 runs may have been some consolation to the Yorkshire crowd.

For this is so very much a Yorkshire ground, fiercely partisan, standing no nonsense, and enjoying to the full every success of its own players. But it is also a ground that is fair to the visitor, warm in its praise of good cricket whoever is playing it.

SCARBOROUGH

THERE is an appropriateness in Scarborough appearing at the end of the sequence of county cricket grounds for it comes into its own towards the end of each season. After the toil and tribulation of the Championship, when the counties have decided on their success or failure, then the real spirit of Festival comes to this delightful seaside town, the players can shake off their heavy responsibilities and maybe for them the real nature of cricket can be enjoyed.

Not that there are no Championship matches here, indeed one may well be included in the Cricket Festival that sees September in, but what Scarborough really stands for is the game which has such a name as Leveson-Gower, T. N. Pearce, The Fenner Trophy, or North and South in its title.

The ground is in the north part of the town, though when it was first used by the Scarborough Cricket Club it was simply a field off North Marine Road. Today there are terraces of tall houses enclosing the east and south sides, giving the not unpleasing character of seaside lodgings. Despite the closeness of the cliffs overlooking the glorious North Bay—and they are within

Scarborough at Festival time.

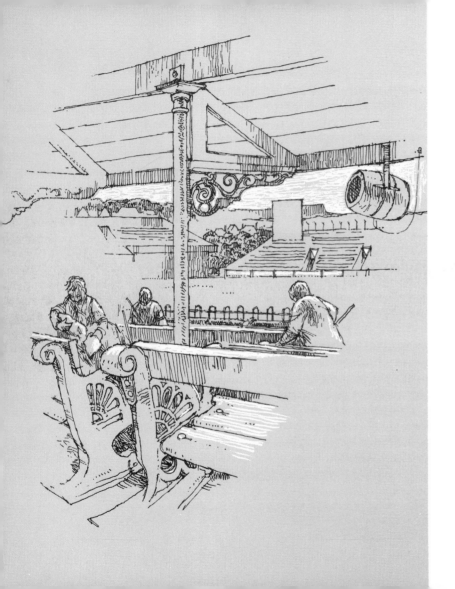

100 yards—the sea is only just visible, from the stands.

But as if to compensate for such a deprivation, the view to the north is magnificent. Away beyond the roofs stretch the moors, their hilltops looking their best in early autumn.

Scarborough Cricket Club was founded in 1849, its early matches being played on Castle Hill, that dramatic promontory which divides the sea into the two bays. By 1863 the present ground had been acquired, and from then on the development was rapid. A professional was appointed in 1873, a pavilion erected the following year—note the order of priority—and in 1876 the Festival was launched with two matches: Scarborough against New Forest Rangers, and Yorkshire against the M.C.C. By 1878 the ground had been purchased for £3,500 and the moment was ripe for further improvements.

In the year that application was made for a County Championship match to be played here another pavilion was built, and in the next year, 1896, the eagerly-awaited first county game took place, which Yorkshire duly won.

Thus, omitting the suspensions because of the two world wars, the Festival has continued. In 1926 it cele-

Looking from the south seating across to the scoreboard, and the moors beyond.

brated its jubilee by the provision of the concrete stand that sweeps round from the pavilion to the scoreboard. It was a considerable improvement, not only for the spectators who could sun themselves all day, but also for the scorers. Their quite magnificent box was positioned virtually over the sightscreen where they enjoy to this day a view of the wicket that must be the envy of all visiting scorers. However it was not until 1972 that the present delightful weather-vane was placed over the tiled roof.

A further stand was built on the west side in 1956, to replace a long, low shelter which earned itself the nickname of the 'cowsheds'; this new west stand has a capacity of 1,800 but nobody would pretend it is beautiful, not even with the creeper growing up its front.

The south side of the ground, that is the Trafalgar Square end, has retained most completely the character associated with the Festival's early years. At the top end, for there is a slope, the tea room has for over half a century served countless spectators, while before that time a refreshment room was provided. A range of shelters, their stepped roofs supported by ornate cast-iron brackets, leads down to the south-west corner of the ground.

It is in this corner that, during the Festival, the tents and marquees are pitched. The centre-piece of them is the flagpole rising from its island of flowers, and next to it the canvas band stand. It is here that the mayor, the cricket club president and other dignitaries hold court. The members take lunch, the players come across from the pavilion, and the town band plays during the intervals. What a scene of cricket's grace and elegance it presents. Tradition survives in a changing world: the singing of "Auld Lang Syne" on the last evening of the Festival against a background of advertisement boundary boards.

In some respects this area of tented 'pomp and circumstance' has its complement on the opposite side of the ground. There the pavilion luxuriates in the sunshine, its rich red brick and tile, its generous bow windows, its hanging flower baskets, all contributing to feelings of solid worthiness and long history—was this really built for only £2,150? But then the first pavilion in 1874 cost a mere £234!

In 1979 the ninety-third Festival was held, so the store of memories here is rich.

Even back in 1871 the matches played were of county standard for when we read of the Earl of Londesborough's XI it meant virtually the Yorkshire XI, and the opponents' title of 'Scarborough Visitors' was another way of saying the leading amateurs from Southern England. Indeed, on the walls of the pavilion's club and dining-room there are photographs of hosts of the amateurs who took part in the Festival.

And it would not be an exaggeration to assert that every county will have had some of its players on this field at one time or another; as for international sides, well they have appeared here since the Aborigines' visit. One might even call this a Test ground, for there has been a One-day Prudential Test Match here.

Despite the sea mist, and the fact that the wicket takes spin, there have been many instances of quick scoring and big hits. It was here that J. B. Hobbs in the Gentlemen versus Players match of 1925 made 266 not out; here that C. I. Thornton playing for the Gentlemen of England v. I Zingari scored 107—eight sixes, and twelve boundaries—in twenty-nine hits, one going for 138 yards into Trafalgar Square. H. Sutcliffe and M. Leyland scored 102 off six consecutive overs in the Essex match of 1932, and in 1952 P. B. H. May, playing for M.C.C. made 174 and 100 not out off Yorkshire.

This is a ground known and loved by the people of Scarborough, the supporters of Yorkshire, by countless holidaymakers, by all who value cricket at its best. Why it might even have been the birthplace of Dame Edith Sitwell, when her mother was attending lunch at the Festival of 1887!

The pleasant weather-vane above the scorebox at Scarborough.

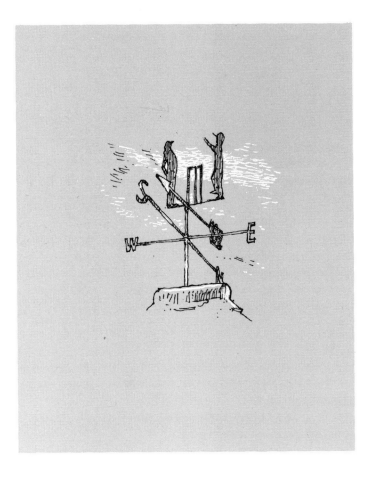

Oxford and Cambridge Universities

THERE are no administrative addresses apart from those of the grounds, the Parks and Fenner's respectively, as the office of secretary changes.

Oxford University Cricket Club was originally known as Magdalen Cricket Club as it played on that part of Cowley Common used by the boys of Magdalen College Choir School. But by 1880 it had moved to the Parks.

Fenner's dates from 1846, but there was a cricket club at Cambridge in at least 1821, for in that year it challenged Oxford to a match. In the event no match took place till 1827, and strangely, since then, the venue has never been at Fenner's.

So far as first-class status is concerned it has been customary for the counties to play the University sides, and indeed Touring teams too have visited both places. But today it is a combined XI which entertains the visitors and the fixture is not regarded as first-class.

Inevitably the demands of the academic year abbreviate the programme, and matches do not continue after June.

Oxford's club colour is obvious, and its emblem derives from the university arms. Cambridge on the other hand relies entirely on its identifiable colour and must be the only team to have a flag bearing nothing on it!

Oxford University
THE PARKS

ANY ACCOUNT of first-class cricket grounds must be considered incomplete unless it includes the university grounds, not only because they have seen many of the great players, amateur and professional, club and international but also because their individuality is evident

---

The fine pavilion at the Parks is echoed by the roof of the University Museum, Keble College Chapel and more modern departments of the University. [following pages]

through their setting.

There could hardly be a better ground for showing the beauty of a cricket field than the Parks at Oxford. Of course it is more than a ground, rather a ground set in a park. When the short season of university cricket ends in June the playing area becomes a collection of tennis courts, and when the summer is over the pavilion stands alone in a landscape of grass and trees.

What trees they are: when the University bought this area piece by piece from 1854 to 1865 the trees were chosen for their appearance in spring and autumn. The splendid avenue of various species which lies to the north of the playing area provides a background that no other ground can hope to emulate. And even with the depredation of elm and beech disease it still remains the finest.

On the east side of the field a line of thorn trees presents a contrast of shape and scale. Their value is more than visual, for they are virtually irreplaceable.

Around the Parks other groups of trees can be seen, each contributing a variation of colour. One of the newest stands to the west, and is known as the Coronation Clump.

Through the windows of the pavilion at Oxford, the glorious trees provide a background unequalled anywhere.

Sadly the number of mature trees around the pavilion has decreased but at least there are a few to show what it was once like.

The pavilion is the focus of this ground, for there are no stands, and the boundary is marked by a rope. The Oxford University Cricket Club played its first game here in 1881, and it is from that year the pavilion dates.

From the outside it is a striking building possessing a wide-awake character with its steeply pitched roof gables and magnificently up-thrusting cupola. Its walls are 2 feet thick and the timbering is rich, particularly in the veranda where the supports are reminiscent of the bridge at Queens' College, Cambridge. In the centre gable the clock is the original. Some change has occurred in the veranda where the east half has been enclosed to provide a press box.

The inside is superb: the Long Room is the baronial hall of university cricket. Its roof has great tie beams, king posts and braces resting on massive stone corbels. At one end is a fireplace, and the walls are beautifully panelled. Like Fenner's the names of Blues are recorded here, the gold lettering gleaming on its oak. The earliest team is of 1827, and that of 1839 is worth noting for it contained only ten players. Beneath this room are the dressing-rooms, complete with pump, together with the beer cellar.

Immediately to the east is what must be called simply

another building; for to give it a precise title is difficult since it has been so many things. It housed the printing press, it was a harness room, here the professionals ate, collecting their meals from the kitchen door, until the official abolition of the division between amateur and professional. Today it accommodates the visitors' dressing-rooms.

In front, the scoreboard, serviceable if elementary, stands on its concrete platform conveniently next to the ice-cream kiosk of a scorebox.

The turf for the table came from Cowley Marsh and was laid by the Hearne brothers. Over the years it has risen because of top dressing but the original quality is still there thanks to gravel base. Perhaps its only violent change was in 1969 when the pitch was dug up as a gesture of protest by the campaigners for stopping the South African Tour. However despite its being done on the Monday night, the wicket was ready for the Wednesday match, even though protestors then had to be removed bodily by the police.

Cambridge may have beaten one touring side last century, Oxford repeated the victory this. In 1949 it was the New Zealanders who were defeated, and Oxford was the only first-class team to do it that season.

It would be invidious, and almost impossible, to list the names of players whose appearance here has been the prelude to county and international cricket; indeed those panels in the Long Room read like a history of the game. Moreover it must not be forgotten that the professionals who were on the staff also brought lustre to the game.

And if Cambridge can show the devotion of its groundsmen in the longevity of their tenure, so can Oxford, for the holder of that position in 1979 had started his service at the Parks in 1931. His responsibilities do not end with cricket, there being, in addition to the tennis, men's hockey on the east side of the square, women's lacrosse on the west, and men's lacrosse on the north.

If the pavilion be richly appointed, the ground luxuriant, the trees idyllic what of the view beyond? In this respect change has dramatically come, and some might say for the worse. The new Clarendon Laboratory of 1948 started the phase, its quasi-Georgian contrasting with the Department of Engineering tower of eight storeys which stand next to that of Nuclear Physics on the west side of the Parks, both products of the 1960s.

But some of the skyline has not changed. The château-like roof of the University Museum rises behind the Department of Biochemistry, and, most prominent of all, the chapel of Keble College still stands aloof in the south-west corner, its red and yellow brick just as startling as it was in 1873 the year it was begun.

Whatever new building may appear, however brash or modern it seems, the distinctive character of the Parks will not change. It will still give to every newly-arrived undergraduate as to every seasoned professional an experience that can be enjoyed nowhere else, and a pride that can be expressed simply by, 'I have played at the Parks.'

Cambridge University
FENNER'S

THE UNIVERSITY cricket ground at Cambridge is not to be found amongst the mellowed stone of the colleges, nor beside the gentle River Cam, but on the south-east of that extensive open space, also devoted to cricket, called Parker's Piece.

Back in 1846 a certain tenant of Caius College, F. P. Fenner, had use of a field on the far side of Gonville Place—significantly named—so that, when the university acquired the ground, 'Fenners' it remained.

Generations of undergraduates have played cricket here, as well as hockey, and football. Until some twenty years ago there was a cinder running track, around the field, three laps to mile, and it possibly was one of the oldest in the country, as well as the most unusual for it was a clockwise circuit.

It would have to be a very old 'alumnus' who knew the pavilion that stood near to the present nearly-roofed scoreboard and press box. But present-day visitors can see where it was, because the University Cricket Club captain of that time presented elm trees to line the carriageway to it from the main gates. Dutch elm disease has attacked them with the unfortunate result that five have had to be felled and others are dying. However in 1979 six still stood as reminders of a past era.

Many more people will remember the pavilion that was at the south, or Gresham Road, end of the ground. Its distinctive high-pitched roof, central chimney stack and dormer door, its elegant wrought-iron verandah and classical balustraded balcony were features that make it memorable. But bomb damage during the Second World War brought its sixty or so years of service to an end.

Now, that part of the ground has another character: that of blocks of flats. Fortunately some of the chestnut trees remain, to soften the angles and in time doubtless they will become as familiar as the other buildings. Whether the vast bulk of the Kelsey Kerridge Sports Hall that stands by the main entrance will ever be assimilated is perhaps less certain.

However some of the older buildings do remain, preserving something of the old Fenner's. The Department

From the new pavilion at Fenner's, Cambridge. [following pages]

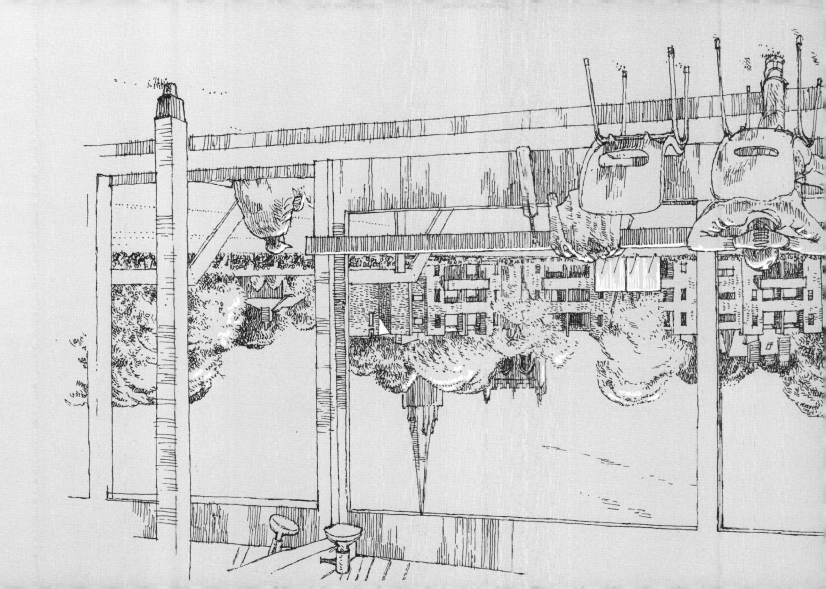

of Human Ecology—a modern enough title—and the University Gymnasium occupy the remainder of that south side, while the tennis courts on the west side still have the sombre hall of the Boys' Brigade. Between the YMCA building and the sports hall there is a glimpse of one of the copper turrets of the University Arms Hotel beyond Parker's Piece.

Most important of all, the tower and spire of the Roman Catholic church still rise behind the flats, to give just that touch of gothic splendour which no cricket field in Cambridge should be without.

There remains the north side of the ground: here the new pavilion, built in 1972, of dark red brick to match the flats, brings Fenner's its own example of modernity. As a building it is innocuous, inevitably lacking the charm and distinction of its predecessor. But it is well-appointed with four dressing-rooms, generous carpeted floorspace, large windows and a terrace for deck chairs. Not everything is new, and it is good to see that the walls of the Long Room bear panels from the old pavilion, recording the 'Blues' since 1827. Many of those early players are listed without initials and interestingly each team is in alphabetical order, so the captain takes his place amongst his players. Even more intriguing is the panel for 1878, or rather panels, for there are two teams listed. The 'Varsity' match had its names commemorated, but so historic was another match that it was decided to record those players too. Surprisingly changes had been made. And what was this second match? Why, against the Australians. And the result? A win for the university by an innings. Such pride surely justified breaking the practice for once.

Eight years before, the 'Varsity' match had had an equally dramatic result. Oxford needed but two runs to win. But F. C. Cobden took the remaining wickets with a hat-trick! The score card can be seen in the pavilion, as can the ball he used. Strangely, there is a similar ball at Lord's!

What does it matter, enough to enjoy the story. Here at Fenner's I'm sure they have the rightful ball. This is a ground that should have all the mementoes it can find. That is why it is to be hoped that the simple wooden stand next to the pavilion will continue to be looked after, for it is perhaps the oldest feature of Fenners.

But then who would want too much change here? Why in the last 120 years there have been only three groundsmen. Yet it is no backwater of cricket, where the play is sub-standard. In the 1949 match against Essex, Dewes and Doggart scored 429 for the second wicket, only twenty-six short of the world record.

Fenner's north end.

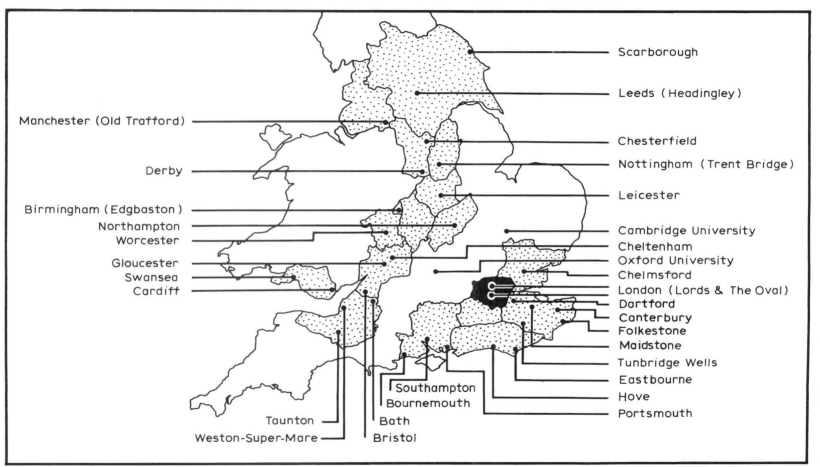

The Counties with the dates they became first-class:
Derbyshire 1873, 1895
Essex 1895
Glamorgan 1921
Gloucestershire 1873
Hampshire 1895
Kent 1873
Lancashire 1873
Leceistershire 1895
Middlesex 1873
Northamptonshire 1905
Nottinghamshire 1873
Somerset 1891
Surrey 1873
Sussex 1873
Warwickshire 1895
Worcestershire 1899 (excepting 1919)
Yorkshire 1873

Bibliography

EVEN A CURSORY glance at the standard source, Padwick, E. W. *A bibliography of cricket*, 1977, will show that few grounds have been written about, and those which have received attention are but the more obvious choices.

The one publication that did attempt comprehensive coverage is now out-of-date, and out-of-print: Yardley, N. and Kilburn, J. *Homes of Sport: Cricket*, 1952.

A year earlier a partial account was given of the four Test Match grounds; Lord's, the Oval, Trent Bridge and Old Trafford, together with a somewhat arbitrary choice of Gloucestershire and Yorkshire, in Meynell, L. *Famous Cricket Grounds*, 1951; while Peebles, I. *Watney book of Test Match Grounds*, 1967, is self-explanatory.

For the rest the literature may be divided into three categories, thus:

(1) full-length books on particular grounds, e.g. Warner, P. F. *Lord's 1787–1945*, 1946; Rait Kerr, D. and Peebles, I. *Lord's 1946–1970*, 1971; Marshall, J. *Headingley*, 1970; Marshall, J. *Old Trafford*, 1971; Palgrave, L. *The story of the Oval and the history of Surrey cricket 1902 to 1948*, 1949;

(2) booklets associated with players' Testimonials, or 'souvenir' type, e.g. Lord's 1979, Hove 1972, Sheffield 1955, Nottingham 1938;

(3) ephemera, e.g. *Green and White—Fenner's observed*, 1962.

And it should also be noted that *Wisden* has in its annual volumes included elementary plans of grounds.

Appendix

The following table shows the pattern of three seasons, 1880, 1930 and 1980, with regard to the range and frequency of the gounds used. Since only matches designated first-class have been mentioned, such competition games as the Gillette Cup, Benson & Hedges, John Player, Fenner Trophy, and Minor Counties have been omitted. Nevertheless it is interesting to observe the changes that have taken place over these fifty-year intervals.

	Derbyshire	Essex	Glamorgan	Gloucestershire	Hampshire	Kent
1880	May Derby (v Aust) June Derby Derby Aug Derby Derby			Aug Clifton (v Aust) Clifton Cheltenham Cheltenham Clifton Clifton	Aug Bournemouth Southampton * (*Antelope Ground)	July Maidstone Tunbridge Wells Tunbridge Wells Aug Canterbury Maidstone
1930	May Derby Chesterfield (v Aust) Derby Ilkeston Burton June Derby Chesterfield Ilkeston July Derby Chesterfield Chesterfield Buxton Aug Derby Chesterfield Derby	May Leyton (v Aust) Leyton Leyton June Leyton Leyton Chelmsford Chelmsford July Colchester Colchester Leyton Leyton Leyton Aug Southend Southend Leyton	May Swansea Cardiff* Pontypridd June Swansea Cardiff Swansea July Cardiff Cardiff Swansea Pontypridd Cardiff Aug Swansea (v Aust) Swansea Cardiff Swansea (*Arms Park)	May Gloucester Bristol Bristol June Bristol Cheltenham July Gloucester Gloucester Bristol Aug Clifton Clifton Cheltenham Cheltenham Cheltenham Cheltenham Bristol (v Aust)	May Portsmouth Southampton Southampton Southampton (v Aust) June Southampton Southampton Portsmouth July Southampton Bournemouth Bournemouth Portsmouth Aug Southampton Portsmouth Bournemouth Bournemouth	May Tunbridge Wells June Tunbridge Wells Tonbridge Tonbridge July Folkestone Folkestone Blackheath Maidstone Maidstone Aug Canterbury Canterbury Dover Dover Canterbury (v Aust) Gravesend Sept Folkestone [Eng XI v Aust]
1980	May Derby Chesterfield (v W.I.) Chesterfield June Derby Chesterfield July Burton Chesterfield Aug Chesterfield Buxton Derby Ilkeston Derby	May Ilford Ilford Chelmsford June Southend Southend July Chelmsford Chelmsford Aug Chelmsford Colchester Colchester Sept Chelmsford	April Swansea May Swansea Cardiff June Swansea Cardiff Cardiff Swansea (v W.I.) July Swansea Cardiff Cardiff Aug Swansea Cardiff	May Bristol Bristol Gloucester June Bristol Bristol July Bristol (v W.I.) Bristol Aug Cheltenham Cheltenham Cheltenham Bristol	May Southampton Bournemouth June Southampton Bournemouth Southampton July Basingstoke Portsmouth Portsmouth Aug Southampton (v Aust) Bournemouth Bournemouth	April Canterbury May Canterbury June Tunbridge Wells Tunbridge Wells Dartford July Maidstone Maidstone Aug Canterbury Canterbury Folkestone Folkestone Sept Canterbury

	Lancashire	Leicestershire	Middlesex	Northamptonshire	Nottinghamshire	Somerset
1880	May Manchester	June Leicester	May Lords		June Nottingham	July Bath
	June Manchester	July Leicester (v Aust)	June Lords		Nottingham	
	Manchester	Aug Leicester	Lords		July Nottingham	
	Manchester		Lords		Nottingham	
	July Manchester		July Lords		Aug Nottingham	
	Aug Manchester					
1930	May Manchester	May Leicester*	April Lords	May Northampton	May Nottingham	May Bath
	Manchester	(v Aust)	May Lords	Peterborough	Nottingham	Taunton
	Liverpool	Leicester	Lords	Kettering	Nottingham	June Taunton
	(v Aust)	Leicester	Lords	June Northampton	Nottingham	Taunton
	Nelson	June Leicester	Lords	Northampton	June Nottingham	July Bath
	Manchester	Leicester	Lords	Northampton	Nottingham	Bath
	June Manchester	Leicester	June Lords (v Aust)	Kettering	Nottingham [and	Taunton
	Manchester	Leicester	Lords	July Northampton	1st Test Match]	Bath
	Manchester	Leicester	Lords	Northampton	July Nottingham	Taunton (v Aust)
	(v Aust)	July Leicester	Lords	Peterborough	Nottingham	Aug Weston-s-Mare
	Manchester	Leicester	Lords [and	Northampton	(v Aust)	Weston-s-Mare
	July Manchester	Leicester	2nd Test Match]	Aug Northampton	Nottingham	Weston-s-Mare
	Manchester	Ashby-de-la-Zouch	July Lords	Northampton	Nottingham	Taunton
	Manchester [and	Aug Leicester	Aug Lords	Northampton	Nottingham	Taunton
	4th Test Match]	Leicester	Lords	(v Aust)	Aug Nottingham	Taunton
	Aug Manchester	Hinckley	Lords	Northampton	Nottingham	
	Liverpool				Nottingham	
	Manchester	(*Aylestone Road)			Nottingham	
1980	April Manchester	April Leicester*	May Lords	May Milton Keynes	April Nottingham	April Taunton
	May Manchester	May Leicester	Lords	(v W.I.)	May Nottingham	May Taunton
	Manchester	(v W.I.)	June Lords	Northampton	Nottingham	Taunton
	Liverpool	Leicester	Lords [and	Northampton	June Nottingham [and	June Bath
	June Manchester	Leicester	2nd Test Match]	June Northampton	1st Test Match]	Bath
	Manchester	June Leicester	July Lords	Northampton	July Nottingham	July Taunton (v W.I.)
	Manchester	Leicester	Lords	Northampton	Nottingham	Taunton
	July Southport	Leicester	Lords	Northampton	Worksop	Aug Weston-s-Mare
	[and Manchester	July Leicester	Aug Lords	July Northampton	Aug Nottingham	Weston-s-Mare
	3rd Test Match)	Leicester	Lords	Aug Northampton	Nottingham	Taunton
	Aug Manchester	Aug Leicester	Lords	Northampton	Cleethorpes	Taunton
	Manchester	Leicester	Uxbridge	Wellingborough	Nottingham	Sept Taunton
	Blackpool	Leicester	[and Lords,	Northampton	(v Aust)	
			Centenary Test		Nottingham	
		(*Grace Road)	v Aust]			

	Surrey	Sussex	Warwickshire	Worcestershire	Yorkshire
1880 June	Oval	June Hove			June Huddersfield
	Oval	July Hove			Sheffield
July	Oval	Hastings			July Sheffield
	Oval	Aug Hove			Sheffield
	[and Gentlemen v	Hove			Aug Sheffield
	Players]	Hove			Sheffield
Aug	Oval	Sept Hove			Huddersfield
	Oval	(v Aust)			Sept Scarborough
	Oval				(v I Zingari)
	Oval				
Sept	[Test Match				
	v Aust]				
1930 April	Oval	May Hove	May Birmingham	April Worcester	May Sheffield
May	Oval	Hove	Birmingham	(v Aust)	(v Aust)
	Oval	June Horsham	Birmingham	May Worcester	Huddersfield
	Oval	Horsham	Birmingham	Worcester	Leeds
	Oval (v Aust)	Hove	Birmingham	June Worcester	Dewsbury
	Oval	Hove	June Birmingham	Dudley	June Bradford
June	Oval	July Hove	Nuneaton	Stourbridge	Leeds
	Oval (v Aust)	Hove	Birmingham	Worcester	Bradford
	Oval	Hove	July Birmingham	Worcester	Sheffield
	Oval	Aug Hove	Birmingham	July Worcester	July Bradford (v Aust)
	Oval	Hastings	Coventry	Worcester	Sheffield
July	Oval	Hastings	Birmingham	Worcester	Harrogate
	Oval	Eastbourne	Aug Birmingham	Aug Worcester	Sheffield
	Oval	Eastbourne	Birmingham	Kidderminster	Hull
	Oval	Hove	(v Aust)	Kidderminster	Leeds [and
Aug	Oval	Hove (v Aust)	Birmingham	Kidderminster	3rd Test Match]
	Oval				Aug Leeds
	Oval				Sheffield
	Oval [and				Bradford
	5th Test Match]				Sept Scarborough

	Surrey		Sussex		Warwickshire		Worcestershire		Yorkshire
1980 April	Oval	May	Hove	May	Birmingham	April	Worcester	May	Leeds
May	Oval		Hove	June	Birmingham	May	Worcester		Middlesborough
	Oval	June	Hove		Nuneaton		(v W.I.)	June	Sheffield
	Oval		Hove (v W.I.)		Birmingham		Worcester		Bradford
June	Oval		Hastings	July	Birmingham		Worcester		Harrogate
	Oval		Hove		Birmingham	June	Worcester	July	Bradford
	Guildford	July	Hove		Birmingham		Worcester		Leeds (v W.I.)
July	Oval [and		Hove	Aug	Birmingham	July	Worcester		Scarborough
	4th Test Match]	Aug	Eastbourne		(v W.I.)		Stourport-on-Severn		Sheffield
Aug	Oval		Eastbourne		Birmingham		Worcester	Aug	Bradford
	Oval (v Aust)		Hove		Coventry	Aug	Worcester		Leeds
	Oval		Hove		Birmingham		Worcester		Leeds [and
Sept	Oval				Birmingham	Sept	Worcester		5th Test Match]
								Sept	Scarborough

The "Cricketers Hotel" which can be seen just outside the ground at St Helen's still provides that Edwardian feature that so many other places have lost.

Index